Positive Reinforcement

TRAINING DOGS IN THE REAL WORLD

Printed and Distributed by T.F.H. Publications, Inc.
Neptune City, NJ

Positive Reinforcement

TRAINING DOGS IN THE REAL WORLD

Brenda Aloff

T.F.H. Publications, Inc.
One TFH Plaza
Third and Union Avenues
Neptune City, NJ 07753

This book has been published with the intent to provide accurate and authoritative information in regard to the subject matter within. While every precaution has been taken in preparation of this book, the publisher and author assume no responsibility for errors or omissions. Neither is any liability assumed for damages resulting from the use of the information herein.

ISBN 0-7938-0525-2

Printed and bound in the United States of America

contents

foreword

Operant conditioning is not a method or technique. It's the law—just like gravity! Just as Newton recorded the "rules" that gravity follows, other researchers have studied behaviour and have set down the rules or patterns that learning follows, as well as studying how environment can affect learning and behaviour. Whether you are aware of it or not, as trainers you are already involved with operant conditioning. No matter what your philosophy, it may behoove you to find out what the rules are so that you can train most effectively!

Behaviour is consequence driven. To be more accurate, I could say that behaviour is driven by **contingency relationships**, which means that stuff happens **before** a behaviour and **after** a behaviour. This relationship between antecedent events (the before stuff), the behaviour, and the consequent events (the after stuff) is what the study of operant conditioning is all about.

I love the British spelling of the word behaviour. (I read a lot of British murder mysteries—love'em.) I cannot remember where I saw it and therefore cannot give proper credit to whomever should have it...But somewhere I saw a sign that said "The most important letter in behaviour is U!" Isn't that great!

introduction

A Note to You, Dear Reader

First, I appreciate the fact that you bought and/or are reading my book. Thank you for caring enough about your dog to educate yourself. Whether or not you like my book or agree with my philosophy, I am glad you took the time to learn more about your friend and mine, the dog.

About Me

(If you aren't curious about me, you can skip this part and go to the bit about my philosophy.)

I have been involved with and lived with animals of several different species all my life. I got my first pony when I was four and was not far away from a stable until after my daughter was born. Fortunately, I had indulgent parents (particularly Mom), because I raised chickens in my bedroom and had, at one time or another, every rodent known to man, as well as cats and dogs. Summers were spent on my pony, with my current cat and dog following. I also had a brief excursion into goats. I just adore goats—very interesting and inventive creatures. As an adult, I took up dogs in a serious way. The horse show circuit is demanding and expensive and by the time my daughter, Abbey, was a two-year-old and an extremely mobile toddler, the shows were dangerous for her. As an infant I could just nurse her between classes and hand her back to one of the trainer's wives, but as every mother knows, a toddler is an entirely different matter! Since I wanted to raise my child myself, I settled down at home to do so. That lasted a whole two years, when I turned my sights to dog shows—Hey! I could load up several dogs and a child and go. I didn't need lots of labor to help me put the cart in the back of the truck, load hay on the top of the trailer, etc. And then Abbey decided to show in the breed ring and do some junior handling. Perfect!

So, basically I am just like you. I have dogs, live with them, and show them. I also have a job, a husband, and a child. Living with multiple dogs and meshing their individual personalities into daily life with humans is most of the time a hoot, sometimes maddening, sometimes frustrating, and sometimes I wonder why I would actually choose to live this way at all, with dog hair festooning my clothes and my meals. You can't even travel without dogs and get away with it. You will be at someone's party in another state, open your luggage, and there it is! A little momento from home. My clothes tend to be less than stylish, because at my house if you can't clean a stall in it, mop up dog waste in it, withstand the onslaught of muddy paws in it, or cuddle a puppy in it, what use is it?

I pretty much was done with horses by 1990 and just have one ancient Morgan mare left. I do miss the horse scene occasionally, but life goes on. I got my first Fox Terrorist, Breanna, and then the fun started. In 1993, I opened a commercial boarding kennel (there's a learning experience for you!) and began to do in-home behaviour counseling. My clients were (and are) mostly by veterinarian referral.

I have not been madly successful in the show ring—in case you are looking for cabinets full of trophies. I originally got my dogs as pets and that is what they are —foremost family dogs. In spite of the fact that they may not be ideal obedience prospects, I continue to work with what I have. This is not a judgement, just what I have chosen to do. The problem solving is what I enjoy rather more than showing. Breanna has had to put up with all of my experimenting with training and is doing utility behaviours. I have done a lot of fiddling and training with the whole house full of dogs as well as client dogs. I also do rescue work and have kept many of "the unplaceables," all of which require behaviour modification of some sort or another. I like to show and enjoyed showing horses and dogs, but have discovered that what I really love is interacting with animals and, in extension, their people. So I will continue to show in the limited fashion that my busy time schedule allows, but up to this point I have not been driven to be a top competitor, nor do I anticipate that happening. I like obedience because it is a vehicle that is available to socialize with other dog people, as well as a way I can relate to my dogs. Quite frankly, the relationship with my dogs exists with or without the obedience ring.

I have done a few seminars and enjoy that kind of work very much. Some involved teaching obedience behaviours and others were about working with aggressive dogs. Aggressive dogs are one of my fascinations—interesting adaptations to the environment occur and aggression is one of them.

In 1996, I got this great idea to do something for pet people. So I conceived of and wrote a program for our local MCTV, Midland, Michigan TV station. The program was called, *So You Think You Want a Dog....* The first of four programs aired for the first time on May 5, 1998. The programs covered useful information for people who might be considering whether or not a dog is a suitable pet for them. They included interviews with different dog experts and breeders and showcased lots of dogs. The shooting took place both in the studio and on location. That was a learning experience! Also included were several little "skits" with dogs in the starring role. Karen Breternitz (the volunteer producer and editor) worked on this project, and it would not have been possible without her endless patience with my foibles and her skill as an editor.

The author gives her Fox Terrier, Breanna, a treat for all her hard work.

Why Reinforcement Training Works

Command-based training or "traditional" training methods rely on physical manipulation of the dog's body to teach. The dog is guided physically, pushed, pulled, and corrected with a choke collar to get the point across. I will not tell you that you cannot train this way; there are hundreds of dogs out there that have been. However, if praise is the only R+ the trainer is utilizing, that trainer is also relying heavily on coercion and punishment (avoidance behaviours). How long do you think you'd go to work for that same old "Good boy," at the end of every week?

Operant conditioning speaks to the dog's mind. You communicate directly with the dog's conscious thought processes. Pretty heady stuff! (No pun intended!) With understanding comes long-term reliability.

Human belief in punishment is very touching, especially in light of how difficult it is to carry out punishment correctly and how unreliable punishment can be in behaviour modification. Humans somehow think that punishment makes behaviour more reliable. But does it really? In my experience, R+ is a much stronger force. But you don't have to believe me. Read a few books about behaviour modification in the learning laboratory. If you can read Murray Sidman's *Coercion and Its Fallout* and remain unchanged by it I would be amazed.

Part of the myth that punishment works best for modifying behaviour, in my humble opinion, is found in the fact that with punishment you do get immediate results. Most often, those results are temporary. It is a given that over time you will need to escalate the punishment to merely maintain the behaviour you wanted, never mind improving the behaviour. And the fallout from that will dig you into a deeper hole than you can climb out of. No lectures, please—I have worked with countless dogs and clients at this juncture and have seen the holes that have been dug with coercion. Some of them are darned hard to fix. The fallout from coercion tends to plague you for a long, long time—and when you least will appreciate it.

With R+, you have what I call the snowball effect—the behaviours begin small and slowly, but as the dog figures out the pieces of the puzzle, the behaviour blossoms and soon there you are! With a whole snowman! And the fun you have building it is an added asset.

Another item humans have a touching faith in is *spoken* language. Please remember that your dog isn't genetically prepared for language acquisition. Period. So repeating the command louder or repeating the command at all will probably not net you the results you wish to obtain. If you have to explain it in words, or a sentence, your dog will never get it.

Learning what dogs are about and truly communicating with them instead of just talking at them can be a great journey. A journey that can change your whole paradigm and the way you look at your world. It has mine. Have fun!

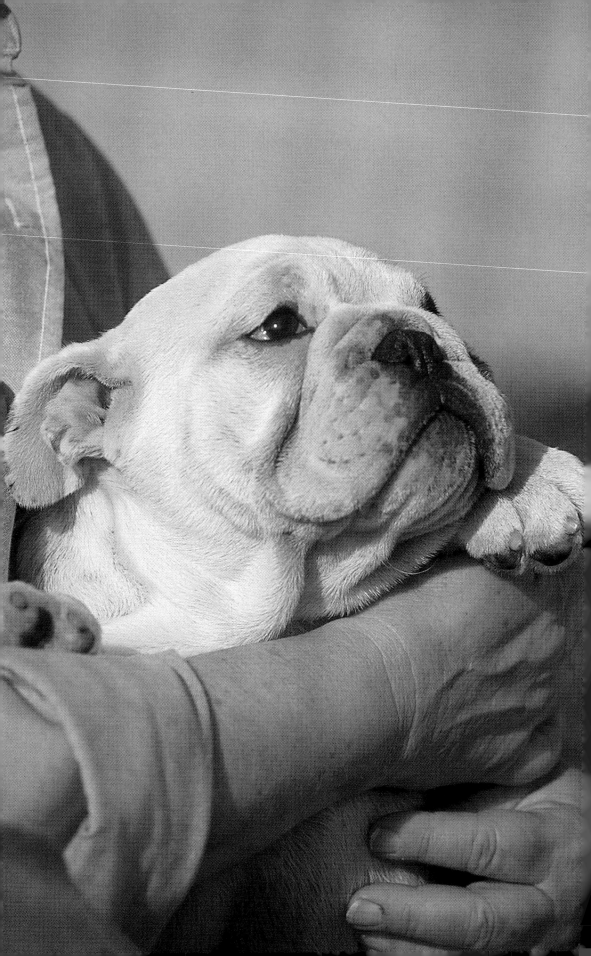

history and terms of operant conditioning

Classical Conditioning

Good old Pavlov, that guy we all learned about in science class (for most of us, this was just a couple of years ago, right?!) knew that dogs salivate when they eat. A pretty common thing for mammal types to do. Well, he also figured out, kind of by accident, that when he paired food with particular consistent stimuli, such as a bell, the dog would salivate when he heard the bell ring, even if the food was not made immediately available. Being intrigued by this, he did further experimentation. The gist of what he learned is this: The dog could be **conditioned** to salivate at the sound of the bell, which had previously caused no response. The salivation happened even when food was not offered or immediately forthcoming. Big deal, you say! Just you wait until you find out what else our dogs can teach us slow, old humans!

By the way, Pavlov named this new discovery **conditioned response**. Salivation was the response to the bell that had been paired with food. The bell becomes the **conditioned reinforcer**. Synonyms for conditioned reinforcer are secondary reinforcer, reward mark, bridge, or event marker. Whatever you call it, they all refer to the same item.

Operant Conditioning

A whole bunch of guys got fascinated with operant conditioning, and you can look their work up in the library if you like. Some of the early Behaviourists were Thorndike, Watson, and Hull—but the guy who did the most advanced research in his day was B. F. Skinner, a Harvard professor. Skinner, through his experiments, learned some basic "constants" about behaviour, and learned behaviours in particular.

- A behaviour or habit will not be learned if the response is never reinforced. This is a basic survival tactic. If an organism wastes a lot of time doing stuff that doesn't work to aid survival, it is soon out of the gene pool.
- A behaviour will be repeated and thus quickly become conditioned (a habit) if it is reinforced.
- Once learned, a behaviour is maintained most efficiently if it is reinforced on a random or intermittent basis, rather than every time. (Believe me, this is the tricky part. This is where the upper echelon of trainers excel. When you get good at this, let me know and share your secrets with me!)

A behaviour or habit will not be learned if the response is never reinforced. Once learned, repetition, instead of food, can maintain the behaviour.

- A behaviour that has been "learned" will quickly become "unlearned" or a better way to put it, I believe, is *unoffered*, if the reinforcement is discontinued. (How quickly this happens depends on the reinforcement schedule that the particular behaviour was dependent upon.)

There, now, you clever dog, you, you have everything you need to know to train any organism to do anything!

Once you become intrigued with this stuff, you will still be learning, relearning, and finding ever new ways to use the principles that I have just set down for you here.

"Wait," you say. "How in the heck do I apply all this stuff?" Good question— with a capital Q! You're right, if it was that easy, everyone would immediately become the world's best trainer effortlessly! Training is a unique blend of science and art.

training concepts

Our dogs are learning all the time. Much of what they learn from us, their human teachers, is unintentionally taught. It is just as easy, perhaps easier, from the dog's point of view, to learn what we humans call "bad" behaviours as it is to learn "good" behaviours. To the dog, it's all just behaviour—there is no morality attached.

The Bad News

A lot of traditional training methods, for dogs, humans, and other organisms, are based on force, coercion, and punishment. Although rewards and praise have sometimes been a part of the training picture, aversive methods of control have usually been the focus. While punishment and force certainly can change some behaviours, the use of coercion as the primary tool to change behaviour is unwarranted in many cases and inappropriate or absolutely unneeded in others. Punishment often creates more problems than it solves. In general, force/punishment has a tendency to suppress all behaviours across the board. The other phenomenon associated with coercion as a method of controlling behaviour is that it looks good up front: You get an immediate response to the punishment—the behaviour stops. However, the suppression of the behaviour is only temporary in the majority of cases. Punishment may be used as a way of getting your "foot in the door," but then you have to train your dog so that a wanted behaviour will take the place of the unwanted behaviour. If you don't, you will find that the old bad behaviour resurfaces again, requiring ever more punishment to suppress it. For example, if you don't like Spot jumping all over guests, teach him to greet guests by sitting for attention. Spot can't sit and jump at the same time—they are mutually exclusive behaviours.

The Good News

There are alternative ways to go about getting the job of training done. Under the rather dull labels of "behavioural sciences" or "learning theory," there is an absolute gold mine of information about how to obtain behaviour you like from virtually anyone—your dog, cat, child, or spouse! It's fun, and it's not difficult to understand. Dogs prefer it, and people prefer it, too. Instead of punishing the infinite variations on a theme that your dog can come up with to do something wrong, choose the one correct behaviour (something you like) in each instance, and reinforce it. A big time saver! Less confusing for the human, less confusing for the dog, and more pleasant for everyone concerned.

Training is a two-way street or loop, where the teacher actually communicates with the pupil. (For me the lines here are blurry—I think both participants assume both roles, depending on who's currently "talking.") An event at one end of the

Training is a two-way street and should ultimately help to form a relationship with your dog that is based on trust, confidence, and respect.

Positive Reinforcement

loop changes events at the other end of the loop. To a real trainer, the responses that the pupil gives are wonderful feedback, even if the behaviour you get isn't quite what you expected. In this manner, the teacher learns as much as the pupil does.

All training involves **learned behaviours**. These are different from **fixed action patterns** (instinctive or inborn behaviours), because they are directly related to the experiences that the animal has as it goes through life.

It is wonderful to have words that describe our actions. People love words, and Skinner and other researchers have designed helpful words for us to use. They elegantly and simply explain exactly what they mean. **Operant conditioning** implies that the operant (trainee) is not just a passive participant, but a partner in the learning process. In dog-training terms borrowed from the Schutzhund field, the dog learns to drive the handler for what he wants, which is the really important step and the heart of positive reinforcement. It implies that the communication loop goes both ways and that the lines are always open. Fear, pain, and coercion will most effectively cut the line of communication and sever the "loop."

Training by **reinforcement** may be called different names: behaviour modification or reinforcement theory. Dog trainers tend to use the term positive reinforcement training. A powerful example of how these methods are applied is in the training of marine mammals (dolphins, killer whales, etc.). I figure if they can teach a killer whale to jump through a hoop, surely by using the same techniques, I can teach my domestic dog to sit in the living room without the use of coercion! Many dog and horse trainers also use positive reinforcement training. Exotic animal trainers certainly rely on positive reinforcement, and it allows them to live longer! Using *only* positive reinforcement, you can train a chicken to dance—think about that feat! The chicken, an animal that cannot be trained by force at all, responds readily to being trained with positive reinforcement. Some human behavioural disorders, such as autism (a form of disorder characterized by withdrawal to all normal stimuli), respond to shaping by reinforcement almost exclusively when other methods have failed.

Timing the reinforcement properly is of the utmost importance. Timing is the real "T" word in training—a great treat poorly timed will get you unsatisfactory results. Poor timing results in **missed associations**. A delayed reinforcement is useless. The animal makes absolutely no connection between the reinforcement and the behaviour. The fault is with the trainer and the latency (lapse between behaviour and consequence) of the reinforcer. Reinforcing behaviour too soon or reinforcing behaviour that has not yet occurred can also slow down the learning process. The message is again lost, because, as with delayed timing, the connection between reinforcement and behaviour is not made. Often with improper timing, the wrong behaviour entirely gets reinforced. For instance, my puppy pees on the rug, and when I walk into the room, the puppy looks up and begins to bounce toward me. At this point, if I yell and grab the puppy, what have I just punished? You got it—bouncing toward me happily, a behaviour that I really want to retain as a recall, not punish. **The consequences must be contingent on the behaviour in a meaningful way for the dog**—or the connection will not be made by Spot. Period!

At this point you may be asking yourself the following questions:

1) Why should I use positive reinforcement?

2) What constitutes a positive reinforcement, anyway?

3) What is all this fixed and intermittent reinforcement stuff that I keep hearing about, and isn't this all getting too complicated? I just want my dog to sit, down, come when called, always be a good dog, bring my slippers, and in general, read my mind. Do we really have to go through all of this? Can't I just swat him a few times with a newspaper and get it done lots quicker? And shaping—isn't that what I do with my mashed potatoes when I want to contact alien beings?

4) Even if, after sorting through all of this scientific jargon, I still wanted to— How do I use positive reinforcement?

The answers are: Because positive reinforcement training works. It is also fun. It builds instead of erodes your relationship. Those of us who are working competition obedience know that attention is everything. With this kind of training, attention is like the oxygen emitted from trees during photosynthesis— a by-product. For you left-brainers or logistician types, it's scientifically proven to be the best way to teach, modify, and retain behaviours in all of us—not just dogs. I personally cannot imagine *not* being aware of the laws of learning. Knowledge of them helps me live better on a daily basis. Finding out about learning theory was like walking down a long hallway of closed doors. Each piece of knowledge I acquired became a key to opening those doors, and now I am running down that corridor and those doors are flying open. So why doesn't everyone use this stuff? Other than the obvious—not knowing about learning theory—I think that many people do not use positives to teach for a few reasons:

Reason #1) You must know more than the pupil, at least about the lesson you're teaching. How many of us train at random, with no clear vision of where we're going? I wouldn't want to take a poll! The results would be scary.

To have vision, you must set goals. The first step in the training process is to know what your goals are! So that means a certain amount of—No—not the "P" word!—Yes—planning. I know it's tough, but there it is. You can't set goals and attain them if you have no inkling of what they are!

You must be prepared to adjust your criteria to the learning speed of the pupil. The pupil determines the means and speed of how he learns a behaviour. When using reinforcement training methods, the trainer admits right up front that the trainee is in control of how quickly he is able to absorb any particular lesson. Many of us find it very difficult to give over that control. (Maybe because of insecurity on our part? Secretly, deep in our bosoms, are we worried that we really can't train this animal to obey our commands?) As the trainer, you must absolutely believe that you can find a way to teach the lesson to the trainee—and you can! Establishing mutual communication is the primary objective in any relationship. By relying on positive reinforcement, this is virtually taken care of for you, which is what this technique is all about: **clear communication**. Positive reinforcement is not about "just flinging food about in a random manner" nor is it about being permissive. Positive reinforcement, or R+, is about selecting behaviour you want to see again. Now you just have to apply the "art" of training, which is the *timing* with which the reinforcer is given. Timing determines what behaviour you will or will not obtain.

One of the most pleasant things about positive reinforcement training is that the trainee will offer you many behaviours that you would otherwise never get to see. Coercion, on the other hand, has a lot of effects, and one of those is suppression of behaviour.

Reason #2) R+ requires the trainer to do a lot of thinking on his or her feet. You must be a good problem solver. I think that people are often just uncertain about how to begin. It is hard to have a pat answer when you don't even know what the question is. Open your mind and educate yourself. I can assure you that you will improve with practice, and your dog will love you for it. This involves the communication "loop" mentioned earlier: You do a behaviour; the dog responds; based on the dog's response, you respond; etc. Training at its best feels very much like a good conversation.

Reason #3) R+ requires you to have the self-control not to lose your temper and vent or project your frustrations on the dog. I am not saying you *won't* lose your temper—I still do. I am not saying that you will not become frustrated using R+—I still do. R+ is not magic, unfortunately. You do need to know yourself well and develop enough self-control to stop before you dig a much deeper hole. Though it may look horrid to you, whatever Spot offers is really not "wrong" or "right" behaviour—it is just behaviour, some of which you may find desirable or undesirable.

Learning not to take training errors personally is very liberating. When I become frustrated and tempted to correct a behaviour out of temper, I have learned to stop, step away from the situation, and re-evaluate my training steps. By concentrating on the scientific method, I can more easily be objective and think it through. That doesn't mean that you need to be robotic. As a matter of fact, I find that I am more passionate than ever, and it's good passion rather than emotion that wastes my time.

R+ also demands that you leave ignorance about communication with another

When you jump into training, you must clearly communicate to your dog the type of behaviour that you want.

species behind. Change is resisted by many, because it can be scary and uncomfortable. But there is so much to gain! Go ahead, be brave. Step outside your comfort zone and expand your horizons! You can do it!

The offering of behaviours other than a **terminal response** behaviour is a question from the animal to you: Well, is this it? How about this? What if I do this? You must quickly choose the behaviours that are either what you want or a step in the right direction. You really need to think about reinforcement training from this point of view: There are many wrong ways to do a particular exercise, but only one right way. Instead of spending all your time correcting the wrong ways, just choose the one right way and reinforce it. When you begin thinking this way, reinforcement training becomes easy. Ask yourself, "Is this the behaviour I want or a step toward the behaviour I want?" If not, don't reinforce it. If it is, celebrate!

What Constitutes An R+ Anyway?

To train, you have two basic choices: You can rely on positive reinforcement or punishment. Reinforcement is defined as a **contingent event** that will cause the behaviour to be repeated again. Both reinforcement and punishment will alter behaviour. Because the journey is as important to me as the end result, I wish to get the training task (whatever it may be) done with the least amount of wear and tear on the dog and on me. I choose to rely heavily on R+. Why?

- R+ strengthens and enhances the pet/owner bond.
- R+ never leads to avoidance or defensive aggression.
- R+ is forgiving (so, I get my timing wrong, all the dog gets is a free cookie).
- R+ emphasizes and concentrates on behaviour you like.
- R+ minimizes confrontation between the trainer and the pupil.
- If you are training to teach, R+ is your big helper. What I have to say will be valuable to you. If you are training to find opportunities to confront and dominate, training is no longer what we are talking about.
- Primary reinforcers (food) are used less as the behaviour is learned.
- Poorly timed R+ slows down training (this was the only "downer" I could come up with about R+), but a poorly timed correction can really wreak havoc with your training program.

Positive reinforcement strengthens and enhances the bond between pet and owner.

What About The Other Stuff?
Aversives—Tools That Decrease Behaviour

Note: Before you begin training, consider carefully whether your goal is to actually decrease a behaviour using an aversive or whether what you really want is to see another desired behaviour instead. The leaping idiot you call your dog that greets you at the door may not require the use of aversives (they hardly ever work well here) to rid yourself of the unwanted behaviour or to directly decrease the jumping. Maybe you need to consider applying R+ to sitting to greet, instead. Even if you do use an aversive to decrease a behaviour, remember that you will have to use R+ to install a desirable behaviour to take the place of the undesired behaviour.

When you understand that all of these "technical" terms come from the learning laboratory and are based in the scientific world, the way that the terminology is used becomes more apparent. For example, the terms reinforcement and punishment describe the basic intent of either increasing or decreasing behaviour, respectively. Then the adjective of positive or negative is added. *The terms positive and negative in learning theory are used in a mathematical way, rather than an emotional way*—they refer literally to addition or subtraction when we are talking about learning theory.

We've discussed positive reinforcement or R+. There is also an item called **negative reinforcement**. In general, negative reinforcement is not remembered as well as R+ is. Negative reinforcement involves an ongoing aversive that can be "turned off" by the appropriate behaviour. Negative reinforcement is much trickier to apply than R+ and is not as effective in the majority of circumstances.

So when training (or modifying behaviour), you can pretty much do one of four things:
- R+ (positive reinforcement, my personal favorite);
- negative reinforcement;
- positive punisment;
- negative punishment.

I suppose now you might appreciate examples of the "four things," because I can remember originally reading these definitions and thinking, "Great, I still don't have a clue."

Training Methods

1) **Positive Reinforcement**—Presenting (adding) something good to increase behaviour:

> A behaviour is increased by presenting something the trainee wishes to have. An example would be giving the dog a treat for coming when called or giving a treat to the dog when (s)he sits instead of jumping up on you.

2) **Negative Reinforcement**—Taking away (subtract) something aversive to increase behaviour:

> An ongoing aversive event is removed when the desired behaviour is performed. For example, using a Halti-head collar correctly—If the dog is walking on a loose leash, the Halti remains inactive. If the dog pulls, the Halti tightens around their cute little disobedient nose; as soon as the dog ceases pulling, the pressure abates. The dog's behaviour—ceasing to pull—turns off or takes away the bad thing, therefore reinforcing walking correctly on a loose leash.

3) **Positive Punisher**—Presenting (adding) something aversive to decrease behaviour:

> The aversive event is presented after the undesired behaviour occurs. For example, kneeing a dog in the chest for jumping. If kneeing the dog in the chest does not decrease the behaviour, it is not technically a punisher. I personally do not use nor approve of this maneuver. Why? For one, it doesn't work. I have clients who have been kneeing their dogs in the chest for quite some time with no result. I also find it offensive in that it is easy to hurt the dog. I prefer ignoring the behaviour so that it extinguishes from lack of attention. On the backside of that, I teach sitting to greet. Period.

4) **Negative Punisher**—Taking away (subtract) something good to decrease behaviour:

> The removal of something the trainee likes after the undesired behaviour occurs. If your dog is jumping on you while you are holding a treat, remove the treat by closing your hand over it and putting it behind your back. (When the dog sits, give him a cookie.) If a puppy bites you while playing tug of war, immediately stop the play and put the toy away for a few minutes. (When the puppy stops biting, you can resume play.) Note: The stuff in parentheses gives you information about how to train—it is R+. The stuff not in parens is the P-.

Punishers and Aversives

A brief word about punishers and aversives. In most instances, punishers are not an appropriate option. If used, they must be backed up with lots of R+. Aversives are anything that Spot would wish to avoid. (Negative reinforcement,

Giving your dog a treat for displaying correct behaviour is an example of using positive reinforcement.

as well as positive and negative punishers, would be classified as aversive.) Punishers are technically defined as a contingent event that *decreases* behaviour.

You can use aversives/punishment to train; however, aversives and punishers rely on **avoidance behaviour** to train. The problem with using avoidance is that what the dog avoids can be unpredictable. Spot may choose to avoid you or use passive resistance to avoid working at all. I have worked with many, many animals that are only too happy to oblige you if what you want is presented in a palatable way. These animals are originally brought to me as "difficult, stubborn, or aggressive." When aversives are overused, they do tend to make one difficult, stubborn, and aggressive. In many cases, ten minutes of R+ works wonders that you cannot attain with aversives. Again, I am not saying R+ is magic, but it can certainly seem like it!

Low frequency use of mild, noninvasive aversives can be extremely helpful in supplying appropriate consequences to your dog. By noninvasive I am talking about things like removing food or use of a no reward mark (NRM), which will be discussed later in detail. An aversive doesn't have to be physically painful or cause mental anguish, though it certainly can and often does. If a punisher is used, the least fall-out occurs with P-. In many situations, a **negative punisher** is very effective. In general, negative punishers are very noninvasive. You simply remove something the dog wishes to have, then apply R+ to the desirable response. For example, if your dog is misbehaving by barking annoyingly at you while you eat a piece of apple pie, remove the attention: Don't look at the dog, don't talk to the dog, and certainly don't give him any of the pie—unless you like the barking! If he persists, you could put him in his crate, thereby preventing any social interaction. When he is quiet, he can come back out and join the group. A treat for being quiet while you eat might even be in order.

Negative reinforcement is a tool that also comes in handy, but needs to be used sparingly and more carefully, because you are generally applying some physical discomfort to the dog. In short, you are relying on the dog to avoid the aversive that you are applying in order to modify behaviour.

Now a brief word about **positive punishers**. These are aversives that you add by physically applying them. There is a time and a place for them, but in my opinion *only* under one circumstance: dealing with deliberate and willful misbehaviour. (Rather tough to determine—what I use as a gauge is how much actual training for this particular behaviour the dog has under his belt. I do not apply an aversive of any kind unless the dog absolutely understands how to avoid having the aversive applied and has made a deliberate choice to go down the "wrong road.") Also, the punisher must immediately cease when appropriate behaviour occurs. I think you can nearly always find a nonforceful means to solve your problem without resorting to coercion. It is interesting to note that, in many cases, the very best form of correction is to do nothing. That's right; ignore the behaviour and don't reinforce it in any way. Miracles can happen this way, and at least you are doing no harm. Sometimes I find it helpful to use the "do nothing approach" for a behaviour while I am trying to figure out what I am going to do. At least then I'm not busy digging a bigger hole that will be harder to get out of while I'm thinking it through.

> Just for your information: As with all technical lingo, those who use it frequently begin to alter the language changing nouns to verbs or using a specific term to cover a broad idea base. The word bridge, for instance, originally a noun, was soon converted to being used as a verb as well: "I am bridging this behaviour." Punishers are used to decrease behaviour. Often the distinction between punishers and negative reinforcement is blurry in the way different people use the terms. Intuitive knowledge about language and the way a word is used in a particular sentence or instance will give you hints about how that person is using that particular term.

Positive punishers are my last choice for modifying behaviour and used only when absolutely necessary and appropriate.

Here are the facts and the laws about punishers—particularly for positive punishers:

- Punishment is strongly associated with the handler.
- Punishment is difficult to execute properly.
- Aversives used with poor timing are not just punishing, they are confusing, do not teach, and are abusive.
- Punishment leads to finer discrimination. For example, have you ever been ticketed for speeding? So you never broke the speed limit again, right? Or do you merely become very careful about when and where you choose to break the speed limit? In dog training, this can mean: Spot doesn't get in the trash—when you're home, that is.
- Punishers can lead to aggression. Let's say that every time I have met you I say hello, then kick you in the shin. After a time or two, you are uninterested in being kicked again. So you are now looking at limited options. You will choose one of the following, depending on your personality. One option is avoidance. If you cannot avoid me entirely (think of your dog—he *has* to live with you), you have two other options. One of those would be flight—really a type of avoidance. Before I get the opportunity to kick you, you can run away. The other option is to fight. Take me out first, then I can't hurt you or make you uncomfortable.
- Punishers only *temporarily* suppress the behaviour you don't want. In addition, fallout from the punishment may cause other behaviour issues. You must train an appropriate response to take the place of the undesired response.
- Punishers suppress all behaviour across the board. Behaviours you *don't* want to be affected may be. If you are sitting at the dining room table conversing with me and I suddenly leap up, bang my fist on the table, and screech "No" at you, have I really given you any idea about what I really *do* want? Have I given you any information about how you could have avoided the punisher in the first place? The answer is no to both questions.
- For punishment to be effective, it must be administered extremely quickly and must be over with before your dog can react to it.

To use punishers properly, these are the rules (apply to other aversives as well):
- Punishers can be used effectively to "get your foot in the door."
- Punishers can be used to temporarily suppress the undesired behaviour.

Use **positive directives** instead of the word "no." Positive directives tell the dog exactly what you don't like, what behaviour you'd rather have, and how to avoid the punisher that will be in their future if they continue on their present course. I train for specific responses to different words so that my dogs know *how* to avoid correction. Words like "leave it," "drop it," "come," "down," etc. can all keep the dog out of trouble. They are all reinforceable behaviours, so you get to apply R+ instead of a punisher. Also, if Spot chooses to persist and does get corrected, at least he knows why it happened. (This is why it is so important for the dog to know how to avoid the punisher. To do that, he must know what you're talking about in the first place.)

Then you can use other behaviour modification protocols to install desired behaviours.

- The punisher must be *immediate.*
- The punisher, ideally, is associated only with the target behaviour itself and absolutely nothing else. **Target behaviour** is the behaviour to be altered or focused on during a behaviour modification program. (Kazdin, *Behaviour Modification in Applied Settings*, 1994.) This can be very difficult to impossible to set up. If you can't be sure of this, better not use the punisher. You will get what is called **unpredictable avoidance response**. This means that the animal associates the punisher with something other than what you wanted him to. Instead of thinking that his whining caused the aversive, the dog avoids going anywhere near the location the punishment occurred, or he avoids the person that doled out the punisher.
- The punisher must occur each and every time the behaviour does. Otherwise you have set the animal up to believe that there is a possibility to be successful, even if only occasionally, with this behaviour you wish to eradicate.
- You must make a big impression with the punisher. This can get icky and sticky. The impression must be so big that the dog will wish to never ever risk having this happen again. Now you must walk a fine line between *too much* and *not enough*. If I have a student who cannot even time the food reward properly, what makes me think he will be able to time a collar correction properly? Nothing. And if he can't time the correction properly, what leads me to believe that he has the judgement to determine how much or not enough?

In many cases, you dig a bigger hole with aversives, particularly positive punishers and some negative reinforcers, than you can fix. In my opinion, you also train in a lot of extraneous material: I ended up having more items to "fix" when I relied on aversives more heavily—items that I don't even have to think about with R+. Why train in problems? I have found this especially true with competition-type exercises. The dog strongly associates the punishers with the exercise, and this can cause many problems for you in the show or obedience ring or the agility field. For instance, instead of performing the retrieve happily, the dog avoids the dumbbell entirely. You can't get the dog to pick up what he won't go near! I have seen a lot of dogs afraid to stay because they have been corrected for breaking. The dog associates staying with being punished, becomes nervous, breaks the stay, and gets punished. If someone would just apply a ton of R+ for staying and gently reposition the dog when he breaks, the dog will gain confidence to complete the stay successfully. Many dogs that are said to be hard to train are merely resistant to the methodology being applied.

I would be extremely wary of applying positive punishers to any sort of behaviour that is interpreted as "aggressive." If you see aggression and return aggression, be aware that you may get escalating aggression back. I don't know about you, but when facing that 120-pound male Rottweiler I am not all that thrilled about escalating aggression. Come to think of it, escalating aggression is not at all pleasant even in terrier-sized packages. If you need assistance with aggressive dogs, you need to see a pet behaviourist who relies on educated, positive methods.

Key Points

- Remember that the negative/positive connotation here is being used in a mathematical way. Positive means you add something and negative means you take away something. Reinforcement means the behaviour increases. Punishment means the behaviour decreases.
- Reinforcement occurs while the behaviour that the trainer wishes to affect is going on. R+: You add something that the trainee wants to have from the trainer (a smile, a touch, a toy, play, access to other desirable behaviours, or food).
- Technically speaking, reinforcement is anything that will increase the probability that the behaviour will occur again.
- R-: The behaviour can "turn off" something you are doing that Spot doesn't like. Negative reinforcement depends on avoidance behaviour. Negative reinforcers are items the trainee wishes to avoid. R- can be as subtle as the absence of praise or the absence of R+. Negative reinforcement is anything

that the subject will work to avoid having happen in the future, and because of this, the probability of the desirable behaviour occurring again is increased. Another way to express this is that the behaviour of the dog can terminate or prevent an aversive event from happening by displaying a certain behaviour.

- P-: You take away something the trainee wants to have. Put the cookie or toy away until you see the undesirable behaviour decrease. For example, you are playing ball with Spot. Spot is extremely excited and is causing grievous damage to your clothing and your person. Put the ball behind your back until Spot sits. You have removed something Spot wishes to have. (Once Spot is sitting, throw the ball. That is the R+ portion.)
- Punishers can be negative or positive, but punishers cause a decrease in the behaviour.
- Be very careful when you apply aversives, and at the very least, *stop digging and think your way out* of the situation instead of relying on *Brute Force*. Maybe the dog is safer in his crate, and you need a pleasant beverage and five minutes to regain your cool.

new tools for training

To Begin...Do You Know Your ABCs?

Before you learned to read, you learned your ABCs. Before you learn to train, guess what? You must learn your ABCs. Hard to believe you've lived your whole life just to get back into kindergarten, isn't it? Well, now that you know the technical definition of R+ and aversives, here are some new tools for training:

A = Antecedent

An antecedent is what happens before the behaviour. Antecedents must be clear and very consistent—the dog may zero in on any one of several movements, noises, or signals that you make; does Spot think the antecedent is the one *you* intend him to think it is? Antecedents are a signal to the animal that a reinforcement opportunity is available. It is important to *isolate* the cue from your other body movements so the dog and you are on the same page. Do this by very deliberately presenting the cue while minimizing other body motions or facial expressions—in other words, hold still and present *only* the intended cue. Practice *without* the dog in front of a mirror until you are able to do so.

B = Behaviour

Take a look at the behaviour offered to you. Is it what you want, or is it a step in the right direction? If so, reinforce it! Work on shaping the frequency, duration, or intensity of the behaviour *one* item at a time. Is it not the behaviour you want? Work on eliciting the behaviour another way, or just plain old try again.

C = Consequences

Dogs learn by association—they associate their behaviour with what happens during and immediately after the behaviour. The only reason to give a signal or cue (antecedent) is to be able to provide appropriate consequences so that the target behaviour will be repeated. Consequences not only affect behaviour, they are also intertwined with whatever else is associated with the consequences—like you, for instance. If you are a good consequence provider, you will be a good trainer. So reinforce those dogs!

First Things First...Will Work For Food

For reinforcement training, the first thing you need is something the dog will work for. A toy, game, praise, touch, pats—all of these items can be used to reinforce behaviour. In animal training, the very best "paycheck" for teaching new behaviours is food. Food is a primary reinforcer; it is required for survival, therefore very powerful indeed. We do not have to teach the dog that this item is reinforcing—he *knows* it is. As a recap: A primary reinforcer is defined as something essential for survival, and food is the easiest for us to offer. (Figure it out; the other essentials are defined as water, air, and sex.)

A= Antecendent–Breanna, the Fox Terrier, is given a signal (cue) to direct her to the desired glove.

B= Behavior–Breanna runs to retrieve the glove.

Breanna finishes the behaviour by presenting the glove. It is a hot day, so Breanna "balances" the glove.

C= Consequence–Breanna gets a reward mark, in the form of a "yes" or a click, while she is holding the glove and a treat when she gives it to the handler.

Initially, food works better than toys and games to teach an exercise because you, the human, can have a lot of control about *where* the food is placed and *when* it is delivered. *Placement and delivery of reinforcement is all-important.* In fact, it is the absolute essence of training. Trainers often call this timing. It is a well-known fact that in training, as in dancing, skating, baseball, and romance, timing is everything.

You can involve **Premack's Principle**, which means you can reinforce a behaviour by giving the dog a cue or permission to do a behaviour you requested first. If your dog performs a good sit/stay, cue him to retrieve his ball or dumbbell. The thing that he *likes* to do becomes the reinforcer for the behaviour he just did. However, Premack behaviours can be tricky to use. Sometimes they are not at all handy when training; for instance, it may not be appropriate to release your dog to play right at that minute. When you *can* take advantage of Premack behaviours, they are extremely effective—so use them. Use your judgment and use all of the options available to you to train.

In the process of manufacturing behaviour, use your judgment and do what works best *for that animal*. (Notice that I am not discussing *you* here—your likes, dislikes, or preferences. I am assuming that the R+ you are working for is to see the behaviour you want. That is what *you* are working for. The animal that you are training decides what he will work for—determining what is reinforcing for that animal is out of your hands.) You know that you will rely heavily on food during the learning phase of any exercise when you are using a fixed reinforcement schedule (FR-1 or 1 behaviour = 1 reinforcement). However, toys, games, and rewards should also be a part of your training repertoire when a variable and unpredictable schedule is required to maintain the behaviour most efficiently.

An important note about choosing reinforcers: People seem to make a lot of assumptions as they go through life. One of these is to assume that they intuitively understand what R+ is for someone else. This is a bit presumptuous, if not downright arrogant. If you work for me all week and at the end of the week I hand you a bag full of buttons (I mean really fantastic buttons)…Hey, *I* find buttons very reinforcing, don't you? Get the picture? Please allow the dog to inform you what he finds R+. How will you know? Well, ask yourself these questions:

1) Did the behaviour increase using the food, ball, game, or whatever consequences you are currently providing?
2) Does touch help as an R+? Some dogs really don't enjoy touch when they are concentrating and working. They prefer food and information. (Come to think of it, when I am concentrating really hard working on the computer, I am not in the mood to be slobbered all over either.) However, if touch is reinforcing to your dog in a training situation—use it. How do you know? Does the dog look like he likes it? Does he move closer to you, maybe maneuvering so you can get the right spot, or does he move or leap away? Maybe your dog likes to be touched, but if it constantly makes him break position and wiggle around, touch may be too distracting when initially teaching a new behaviour.

My little Smooth Fox "Terrorist," Punch, detests being petted on the head and shoulders when in training situations. She ducks and weaves and squints her eyes at me. At night on the sofa she is Miss Cuddle Bunny and enjoys all kinds of touch anywhere, including her head and shoulders, but when she is working for reinforcement opportunities, she just wants food as a paycheck, with the occasional game thrown in. She also loves it when I jump up and down like an idiot and clap my hands. She tends to join in on this game. I see many dogs that are made a bit uncomfortable about having people bend over them. I don't think this is a rank order issue; I think they just don't like it. Breanna, another of my Smoothies, also wants food, but is uninterested in games. My German Shepherd Dog, Maeve, finds cues themselves reinforcing. She adores it when I tell her what I would like her to do next. To her, games, toys, and food are all a kick. She is a workaholic. Sherman, one of my male Smoothies, could nearly be trained exclusively with touch and approval. He is blatant about how much he loves touch. He is truly Mr. Magic Moment, gazing lovingly into my eyes whenever I touch him. Find out what your dog responds to and use it.

Using Food

Find a food your dog likes—I mean, *loves*. I don't generally mess about with little bits of kibble. I cook up pasta or cut up tiny pieces of cheese, little pieces of bread, or last night's steak dinner. Little bits of cat food work well, too. I prefer something healthy and nutritious. Homemade liver treats are great, but are not all that great for you if you're spitting food at your dog. Many dogs will work for pieces of carrots or apples. In my experience, it works best to have a variety of foods available; this helps the dog remain eager and helps to avoid satiation (which is discussed later in the chapter). The dog doesn't know if this time it's the same old stuff, or maybe this time it is my very favorite stuff. Here's a list of foods you can try:

- Dog kibble
- Dried banana chips
- Dried apples
- Cheese
- Bread
- Croutons (lots of great flavors)
- Squeeze cheese (works really well for scent articles and dumbbell work)
- Fresh cut apples or carrots
- Oinker roll, rollover, etc.
- Deli turkey, ham, etc.
- Cat treats (because of the food coloring/preservatives in the moist treats, I use them very sparingly)
- Any kind of pasta that is the right size and easy to handle; cook it al dente (that means kind of "stiff," not mushy). You can find bags of tortellini at the grocery, either frozen or dried. These are stuffed pasta. Fast and easy to fix up.
- Steak, chicken, etc. (from last night's dinner)
- Dry cereals, etc.

- Homemade dog biscuits, or cut up the pancakes the kids didn't eat at breakfast. (Also, see the recipe in the Appendix for the homemade dog treats.)
- For jackpots, I will use tiny cans of cat food or tuna fish. I can have them in a pocket or in the training bag and whip them out like a conjurer. (Remember Bullwinkle?: "Nothing up my sleeve....")

I usually avoid many commercial dog treats because they tend to have lots of sugar (just what your hyperactive puppy needs—not!), salt, food coloring, and preservatives in them that I don't want to feed my dogs. Also, many of them don't readily lend themselves to being broken into tiny pieces. If you want to use hot dogs, I suggest you soak them overnight in water to rid them of some of the salt and nitrates.

When using food, use your judgment. When trying out new foods, use them sparingly the first few times so that your dog's system can acclimate. I feed a raw, natural diet and a wide variety of foods all of the time, so my dogs' systems are not easily thrown off by trying new foods. Use common sense.

An important note: Training treats are about one-half the size of your little fingernail for most dogs. The size is important because you want to get in as many trials as possible in each training session. I don't want to stand and watch the dog eat—I want to train. Since a big part of training is repetition, and since I don't have much time, I use tiny pieces of food.

Another reason to use small treats is to avoid the evils of satiation. That means that the dog has had so much of something that it is no longer reinforcing at that particular time—like right after a big, groaning meal at the best restaurant in town you don't feel like stopping off for a hamburger on the way home. So you don't have to deal with satiation, use small treats, train in short time frames, and begin with a hungry dog, rather than one that has just inhaled vast quantities of dog food. Also,

Most dogs will work for food. Your dog's favorite treat can be an excellent training motivator.

keep your dog on a feeding schedule.

At this juncture, I can hear you screaming: "But Tina is fat," "But George has allergies," or my personal favorite, "My dog doesn't like food." Obviously, you must follow your vet's instructions as far as food intake is concerned. However, as aforementioned, food is a primary reinforcer and therefore necessary for survival, so we can assume that the dog must eat at some point. Use whatever you can. The special kibble or dog food you must feed may be used. The dog can certainly work for his dinner. Usually there are two or three foods a dog can tolerate. For overweight dogs—less dinner and more exercise. (A regimen that I see in my own personal future as well. Alas, age and gravity...) There are no more excuses. You also can use play, games, toys, touch, social approval, and the appropriate food. Now, go train your dog.

An Extra Helper—Reward Marks

The second item in your bag of training tricks is a **secondary** or **conditioned reinforcer.** Some trainers call this a **bridge**. I like that term because it tells the story. The secondary reinforcer literally bridges the time span between your initiating the bridge and the time when you actually give the dog the primary reinforcer. When instructing classes, I usually refer to a **reward mark**. That also tells the story. You are marking the behaviour or event that will earn the R+ (positive reinforcement). The reward mark (RM) also gives the animal very precise information. It tells the animal, "Yes—what you are doing *right now*— that's what I like" The animal really likes receiving this precise information. All of us, animal and human alike, hate to be confused and frustrated.

The use of an RM is at the heart of training with R+. When I begin to talk about the use of RM (reward mark) and NRM (no reward mark), I am often met with a temporary glazing over of the eyes from the recipients of my conversation. But it is so much easier than you think. What an RM really does is buy you time. It marks the behaviour while you get the treat out of your pocket or from across the room. It becomes an integral part of a communication system. And very importantly, an RM gets you away from having to use a food treat all the time. That's it folks—it's not a difficult concept. More to the point, it involves you changing your own behaviour. That is, you must be very deliberate about what behaviour you mark. Then you must develop the habit of using the clicker or word that will serve as your reward mark. On average, my student's dogs pick up on the RM thing in about 20-30 seconds. It takes my humans *much* longer.

You must reinforce the behaviours you want *exactly* at the moment they are occurring or within a half second for optimum learning to occur. We want to relay information in the most concise way possible to our animals, and it is a bit challenging to pop a treat in the mouth of the dog in the middle of the high jump. So, now what? A reward mark is how you tell animals that are at a distance, or in other situations where immediate delivery of a primary reinforcer would be awkward, that they are on the right track. (Remember Pavlov and the bell?) For example, marine mammal trainers often use a whistle to signal to Flipper that what he did was the right thing, and a fish reward is now available. A reward mark can communicate promptly and clearly what part of the behaviour sequence you were especially pleased with. It should be noted that an RM has less impact or lasting effect than a primary reinforcer (PR), so it needs to be "paired" with a PR periodically, to keep it strong and "charged" up (just like your cell phone).

Rather than thinking of a reward mark as meaning "good dog," think about the RM as being a camera. You, the trainer, will use the RM to signal to the animal right at that exact moment when you have the perfect picture of the behaviour you want to see repeated. As you see Spot's elbows hit the ground when you say "Down," mark it by saying, "Yes!" or with a "click." You then have the option of following up with food or access to other R+ or not, depending on which stage of learning Spot is in. No matter what consequence you choose to provide, when you use an RM, the dog understands what behaviour turned on the cookie machine (that's you).

Using Reward Marks

Enough already—what can I use as a reward mark? Is it expensive? It is a lot of money—that's what all this is leading up to, isn't it? As the old saying goes "the best things in life are free," and reward marks fall into that category. You just open your mouth and say them.

To have a successful RM, requirements must be met. You can use a word or a specific touch. As discussed, marine mammal trainers customarily use a whistle to bridge. Many dog trainers use a clicker, which

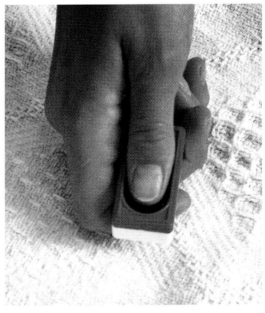

A "clicker," shown here, works well as a Reward Mark because it makes a sound that is unique to the dog's environment.

is a child's toy that makes a click-click sound like a cricket. A clicker works exceptionally well because it is a unique sound in the animal's environment; therefore, it carries a lot more meaning to the animal than yet another word falling around their ears. I have several RMs for my dogs—some key words like yes, good, wow, and excellent. Words are cheap, handy, and always available. I also use a clicker, which is also inexpensive. I tend to use the clicker when teaching very new behaviours, because I can be really precise with it. From another standpoint, using the clicker has also made me much more aware of my timing and precisely what behaviour I am marking. Words come in handy on those occasions when a clicker is not immediately accessible. Another reason that the clicker is so effective is that it is absolutely, definitively consistent. It never portrays frustration or anger, and it never gets tired or sounds sarcastic. It always gives quick and precise information—just what the dog is looking for.

Before long, the information provided by the RM becomes at least as important to the animal as the primary reinforcer that may eventually follow. Many animals get a kick out of the information itself, to the point that they work for the information alone for extended periods of time. Think about it: Don't you love it when people communicate effectively with you? I enjoy it when friends or others whom I respect tell me that I have done a great job. When I have directions to go somewhere unfamiliar to me, I am much happier if I am given landmarks in addition to the directions. Landmarks are very reinforcing when you see them. If I know I will make a turn on the corner just after the neon pink house with black shutters, I feel good as soon as I spot that house, because I know I am on the right track. Very R+! Contrast that feeling with the frustration and often angry emotions that accompany poor directions or hazy communication, followed by punishment when you didn't get it. Or think of the boss who tells you to complete a task. You do exactly what he tells you to do—that is, your perception of what he says—and then you get into trouble because he says you didn't do it right. This does not make you feel kindly toward the boss. Is information a big deal and important? You bet it is—to all of us.

Installing Your Reward Mark

You don't have to install a primary reinforcer, but you do have to install a reward mark. The RM is technically defined as a signal previously meaningless to the animal that becomes meaningful by pairing it with a primary reinforcer.

Installing an RM is just too easy. Begin in a area free of distractions, because this is the learning stage. To make the RM meaningful, cut up about 40 tiny goodies (your primary reinforcer) to about half the size of your little fingernail. (I keep repeating this because invariably I explain all of this, ask my client to go get

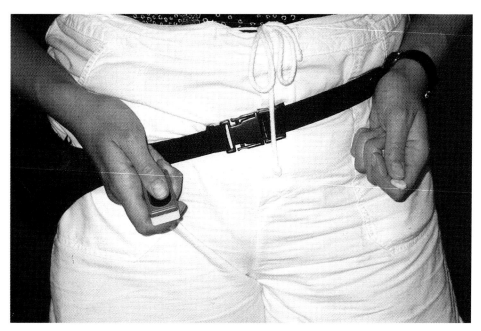

To install a Reward Mark, start with a clicker or a verbal RM like, "yes" and about 40 pieces of your dog's favorite food, cut into small pieces.

training treats, and he comes back with Milk Bones™ for large dogs!) Then make the sound of your RM and give a treat right away. You can clicker train the animal by doing click-treat, click-treat, about 10 to 40 times. If you are using a word as your RM , such as "Yes," the syntax is "Yes"-treat, "Yes"-treat. Don't attempt to actually teach or shape any behaviours at this time. Your goal is for the pupil to associate the RM with food. Move around the room or training area. (If you are outside, please make sure that the dog is safe by using leashes, fences, etc.) Soon Spot will look at you expectantly every time he hears the sound of the RM. You can test to see if Spot is "getting it" by allowing him to wander into the other room or to become slightly distracted, then "click." If Spot immediately looks at you expecting his goodie, he gets it. In place of the "click" from the clicker, substitute any word or specific touch or posture that you want to use as a bridge.

For my dog, Punch, the clicker is a favorite reinforcer. Punch is absolutely fascinated by clickers, and I must hide them from her. Otherwise she steals them and hides them in her crate or carries them around the house, prancing proudly. Oh, there is a drawback of R+: When my dogs hear me working with someone else, they protest because they wish to be included. They can't believe that "so-and-so" instead of *me* is getting opportunities to earn R+. If you are bright, you will R+ those dogs you aren't working currently as well. If mine are quiet in their crates, I remember to pop them a cookie every once in a while, too. Better yet, have others who are walking by the crate "cookie" your dog occasionally. This

While your dog's attention is on you, make the sound of your Reward Mark with your clicker.

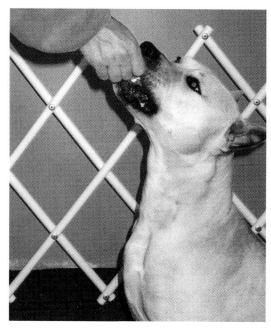

After you present your Reward Mark, deliver your food treat immediately. Your dog will soon form a mental bridge between the sound of the Reward Mark and the food treat that follows.

way Spot receives R+ for exhibiting self-control and waiting patiently for his return.

Touch, expression, tone of voice, consistent signals—these are all additional RMs that we can take into the obedience ring with us. So even though we can't take our primary reinforcer, food, with us, we have a lot to offer Spot in the way of support in the obedience ring or in daily life. I have found that I, and most people, tend to become very reliant on the primary reinforcer, almost more than the dog. Careful planning and management of a reinforcement schedule is where many people fail.

A Short Review

- Bridge, secondary reinforcer, conditioned reinforcer, event marker, reward mark—they all mean the same thing.
- You will use the bridge as an event marker to help Spot remember the behaviour so he can do it again.
- Think of your clicker or word as a camera. You are using it to "snap a picture" of the behaviour you want.
- Timing is very important here: The syntax must always be click, then the goodie. Once Spot knows that "click" means treat, you may then

begin to prolong goodie delivery for up to five seconds.

- You can train any animal to respond to a reward mark. I have several words (yes, good, excellent, clever, wow), plus a clicker that I use as RMs.
- Clickers are great RMs, particularly for beginners, because they provide consistency. You never fail to make the right sound with a clicker, and you never confuse the animal. The clicker makes the same sound all the time and is never tired or frustrated or grumpy.

Happy bridging!

The No Reward Mark

The other very important basic tool in your training bag is called a **no reward mark** (NRM). The no reward mark, which means "give me some other behaviour, because that wasn't it and you will get no cookies from me," may take two or three days or a week to develop. Perhaps a better way to express this is in the number of trials—you're talking about 20-40 trials for the average dog.

So why should I use this, you may ask? This is just getting to be too many things for me to remember. I mean, it would just be easier if this dog spoke English? Yes, wouldn't it though! But dogs don't speak English, German, French, Swahili, or Latin. Considering how often we bungle verbal communication with other humans, I wonder how much help language would actually be.

For many training errors, you want to be able to convey information to your dog without inhibiting his behaviour. Think about this scenario. You are on a biking tour. You come to a fork in the road. You are unsure of which direction to take to get to the right place. So you choose the left fork and pedal about 10 miles. You meet a pedestrian

Scolding is not considered an effective No Reward Mark. You should always use a neutral tone of voice and relaxed body language when correcting your dog's behaviour.

and inquire, "Is this the road to the right place?" "No," he replies. "This is the road to wrong place." Wouldn't it have been great if there had been a sign at the fork? Or even if you could have met that pedestrian 10 feet down the road instead of 10 miles along! The NRM can serve as a sign, a great way for Spot to understand, "Don't go down that road! Offer me some other behaviour." Using an NRM is one way you can give your dog *twice* as much information than if you use only a reward mark (RM).

The NRM is not intended to be used in conjunction with any sort of physical punishment. In fact, the word you choose should be uttered in a very neutral fashion. The NRM is used to convey information to your dog. It is not used to convey disappointment or anger directed toward the animal.

Let's say you are at the department store, and you are looking at accessories, perhaps a scarf to go with your new suit. If the salesperson pulled out a scarf you didn't want to purchase, would you scream "No!" and seize this hapless individual by the throat, shake her, or pinch her ears? (Even if she should have *known* this color is not becoming on you!) If you would, let me please suggest the following strategy: How about responding with, "Not quite. Do you have another I could peruse?" This is the function that the NRM should also serve. It is a way to use a much milder aversive as a means of communication, rather than resorting immediately to physical punishment as a resolution.

Installing the NRM

Choose a word. Don't use "no," because most dogs have been "no-ed" to death. In my household "No!" is reserved for situations where "if you do that again, Spot, life as you know it will cease to be." My NRM is "Too bad." Some of my students prefer "Try again," "Wrong," "Sorry," or "Ah-ah." Doesn't matter—you can say chocolate pudding if you like—just be consistent. You must use a neutral tone of voice for your NRM. If you cannot maintain your temper, you are much better off not using an NRM at all. Or better yet, take a break and come back to training when you have control of yourself. This word is used only to provide information for your dog. It is important to keep your cool and to remain nonthreatening in both tone and body posture.

You can install the NRM separately utilizing food, or you can do what I usually do: Install it on the fly. To install the NRM on the fly, just start using it. Your dog will pick up on it after he has experienced enough trials to establish the pattern. You can tell from the disappointed look on Spot's face and the offering of other behaviour that he is beginning to understand the NRM.

The offering of other behaviour may be extremely subtle. Let's say I have asked Breanna to place herself in heel position and she lines up a bit crooked. If I tell her

"Too bad—pause—"Heel," she will shift her bottom to adjust herself to sit straight. I now have the opportunity to nail the desirable behaviour with an RM and other R+. I have often had dogs that have offered me a down and it is not the behaviour I am looking for. On the occasion that they understand an NRM and I tell them "Too bad," it is not uncommon for them to go from a sphinx-type down (on their chest, elbows down and hind legs tucked up underneath their body) to rolling over on one hip. So look for the subtle communications Spot is offering you in an effort to communicate with this large, bumbling, two-legged, higher primate-like creature. (For those of you in competition, I do not say "Sit straight," and I will explain why. I want a dog that performs a straight sit at heel on the command "Heel." I am not interested in a dog that sits at heel, then waits for my "Sit straight" command to adjust himself. So I tell him "Too bad" to indicate that the crooked sit at heel was not what I was looking for. I repeat the cue for the behaviour I do want, in this case "Heel," so my dog has a chance to correct his position. If I still don't get what I want, or I have to use an NRM more than once, I will review heel position with the dog as a reminder about where heel is.) If need be, use prompts such as a lure or whatever other prompt would be appropriate to manufacture the desirable behaviour *after* you use the NRM. Just remember your timing and do not relinquish the goodie until you see the behaviour you want. In essence, help Spot to try again—he might not have a clue what you want.

Using an RM/NRM is kind of like playing the children's game of "Hot and Cold." If you are unfamiliar with this game, here it is: Someone hides an object. The "it" begins looking for the hidden object. The "director" may give directions in the form of "hot" (getting closer) and "cold" (don't go there—waste of time). Think how much less efficient the game would be if you used only hot or only cold. If your dog is near the behaviour or taking a step in the right direction, then RM; if not, NRM. It is amazing how much work you can get done with the use of these two little words. Clear communication is the name of the game.

How to Install the NRM with Food

In addition to the above technique, you may also use the same steps that you would to teach "leave it." Place a bit of goody on the floor. When Spot goes for it, quickly cover it with your hand and say your NRM. Then uncover the food. If Spot goes for it again, cover the food with your hand again. Ignore any barking, nibbling, sniffing, etc. Do, of course, stop Spot if he becomes too rough and is hurting you, perhaps by crating him for two or three minutes until he calms down. Then begin another trial. When Spot indicates that he is not going to grab the food, you may pick it up, use your RM, "Yes," and give it to him. Please notice the "pick it up" part; in this particular instance, I wish to give the food to the dog,

Using a reward mark—no reward mark system is like playing a game of hot and cold. A good information system is the key to communicating with your dog.

not allow him to get it off the floor. This makes a difference in the dog's mind. Giving the dog the food from my hand is making the communication much clearer, and it is also then very obvious to Spot that the food has become available by use of the RM. How do you know Spot does not wish to pick the food up? He will cease diving at the food. He may even back up a step, turn his head away from the food, or flick his eyes away from the food for a moment. Some animals will walk away.

It might work this way: Spot sort of knows sit in *most* instances. I say "Sit," and Spot gets distracted and doesn't comply. Maybe he looks away instead. "Too bad," I say, and then begin another trial, "Sit." This time I help Spot comply. When I get the sit, I give him a cookie. This is an invaluable addition to your bag of tricks. It helps correct minor errors and moves unwanted behaviours toward extinction. The no reward mark becomes a gentle reminder for the dog to pay attention because soon he may earn reinforcements.

Corrections

Yes, even I use corrections under certain circumstances. There is a point at which I will correct. I make the judgment on a case-by-case basis. Coming when called, for instance, has rigid requirements, and I will introduce correction as required to obtain results (only after I am certain the dog absolutely understands how to avoid the punishment). A poor response to a recall may cost the dog his life.

For competitive obedience exercises when just my ego is at stake, I use

When installing food as a Reward Mark, place it in front of your dog, but do not allow him to take it until you give it to him. Jake the puppy gets a treat for being patient.

almost no corrections beyond an NRM. This is an ethical decision each one of us must make for ourselves. I feel the best about myself when I rely heavily on R+. If I am in a situation where I have to correct my dog, I know the event indicates a lack of training—guess who is responsible for that? I long ago gave up the mind set that I *have* to do anything, much less correct my dog! I always have options, and I can always punish if I am backed into some sort of training corner. But the question I ask myself is this: **Have I really explored all of the training options available?** Have I taken the time to train the exercise properly? Am I absolutely, unequivocally certain that this is willful disobedience on the part of the dog? How can I be certain of that? I do not allow myself to punish out of anger or frustration—and those times are when I am most tempted. When I am frustrated with my inability to communicate properly, that is when physical punishment is tempting. I have decided that if I get frustrated, I put it all away until a later time. Give yourself and your dog or moment (or a day) to de-stress. Get a plan together to handle the training issue and walk away from it for right now. Piling worse on top of bad will not solve any problems.

Summary for RM/NRM

- The NRM is a signal to the dog that whatever behaviour just happened will result in no reinforcement.
- Do you remember playing the Hot/Cold game as a kid? Every Easter my mom and dad always played this game with me during our Easter egg hunt. Think of using the RM/NRM in the same way as playing the Hot/Cold game with your dog. Using an RM and an NRM, you are able to give the animal twice the information.

other tools to develop behaviour

Opportunity Training

Behaviour that is already occurring naturally with Spot can be positively reinforced each time the trainer sees it. It will become ever more likely that the behaviour will occur again. An example would be that your new puppy comes over to you while you are walking around the house. You smile and maybe play, pet, or even pop him a cookie. Just this action alone will make the puppy coming to you more reliable. I like to call this **opportunity training.** When opportunity knocks—notice and reinforce it! This is a great way to elicit many behaviours. If someone is polite to you, you warmly say, "Thank you." This is a positive reinforcement for being polite. If you like your girlfriend's new haircut you say "Girlfriend, cool new 'do." This is R+ for your friend to look good. If you get good grades and your parents respond with a dollar for each "A," that is positive motivation for getting more good grades. If your dog is chewing on his own toys, instead of your new (on sale and still expensive) leather loafers, saying "Good baby" in a sweet tone of voice will convey your approval to your pet.

Shaping

Shaping—It's not what you do with your mashed potatoes, it's baby steps, baby steps, baby steps to success. **Shaping** is a process that you can use to change behaviour. The technical term for shaping is **successive approximation**. This means you teach a behaviour in step-by-step increments, just like you learned to count, then to add, and then to multiply. You take a behaviour that looks like it is a step in the right direction and R+ it. Shaping aids you in manufacturing a

terminal response behaviour that the animal might not offer up on its own. Sometimes the idea just won't occur to the dog without some help, so you begin by applying R+ to those behaviours that are a step in the right direction. By picking and choosing out of what is offered, you can effectively alter the topography (appearance) of the behaviour. Want a quicker recall? First reinforce the dog every time he comes to you, solicited or offered. Then R+ only those recalls preceded by your cue to come and then only those that are within a given time frame. If the dog normally comes in at a walk, manufacture moving toward you more quickly (run when the dog moves toward you, toss a ball as the dog begins to move toward you, etc.) Then reinforce only those recalls when the dog trots or gallops in—don't R+ those "walk-in" recalls. Get the picture? You break down each task into small and easily digestible steps, building the next step upon the previous one. While it sounds complicated and some long behaviour chains can be quite involved, it is my experience that the end result actually comes along very quickly. At the same time, you are making each "link" of that behaviour "chain" strong and resistant to breaking.

Shaping Behaviours— Some Suggestions

1) Break each task down into small steps. This way, Spot gets lots of chances for R+ and is less likely to give up. He will keep trying to offer behaviours in order to get the reinforcement. This makes it easier to succeed at the exercise, which is encouraging for you and for Spot. Remember that success for the dog translates into success for you. It also makes each link of the chain strong. I make paper ladders for all my behaviours in order to keep myself on track. (Paper

You can shape your dog's behaviour by breaking down each training task into small steps. Dervish is learning how to answer the door properly.

Train your dog to do one behaviour at a time and then string the correct behaviours into a sequence. The presentation is only one behaviour in a retrieving sequence.

ladders are flowcharts for a behaviour. They show you where you've been, where you're going, and how you're going to get there. They give you information for future trials about what worked and what didn't and insight into perhaps why.) I can also track my progress over a period of time, which can be very comforting on those occasional off days. It is then easy to see how many actual trials you have done with this particular animal and exercise. For example, you started teaching the drop on recall six months ago. Why doesn't this dog get it by now? By looking at your ladder, you see that in six months you've only worked on the drop on recall for 4 sessions out of a total of maybe 12 trials. Well, that shows you Spot's point of view—and pinpoints who may need to work on what!

2) Train for only one behaviour a at a time. To change the topography (or appearance) of a behaviour, you can alter the frequency, intensity, or duration. If my end goal is a behaviour chain or sequence, I will train each "link" separately, then string all the behaviours together when each individual behavior is being performed correctly by itself. For instance, if I want my dog to bring a dumbbell back to me over a jump, I would train the jumping separately from the retrieve. In addition, I would break the retrieve itself down into many separate steps.

3) When introducing a new step, temporarily relax your requirements for the old steps. If you increase the duration of your sit/stay, you will decrease the distance, for example.

When introducing a "new" criteria, like greater distance to your sit/stay, you should temporarily relax the old criteria. Then you should gradually increase the old criteria at the new distance.

4) Plan your program carefully so that you stay ahead of your pupil. Have your goals clearly in mind and your steps and criteria planned out. Yes, right-brainers and left-brainers alike, make ladders and write it all down! I cannot emphasize this enough. Looking back over the chart will show you Spot's real progress rather than your imagined progress, pointing out how much you and your partner really have accomplished. It will also bolster your spirits on those dark training days when nothing is going right.

5) If a behaviour begins to deteriorate or fall apart, go back to kindergarten. That means you begin at the beginning again and review the whole process with easy reinforcements. Reviews always go much more quickly than the original training process and really help the dog—so don't hesitate to review!

6) If the procedure you are using does not get results, try to get the behaviour some other way. Creativity is a big part of training. Helping the pupil to understand what you want is an art, not a science! It depends on how well the trainer can think of different ways to convey to the student what he wants, or how good the trainer is at breaking the behaviour down into

These chutes prompt the dog to do the correct behaviour so that the trainer can reinforce it.

smaller steps. You would be astonished at how small you can break each step down. A down/stay begins with one second and eventually works up to the 45 minutes you require to set the table and eat dinner.

7) End each session on a high note. Always quit while you're ahead! I learned this training horses, and I always found it the most difficult part of training. I would go so far as to say that the difference between a good trainer and a great trainer is knowing when to leave a behaviour alone and come back to it later. Also, changing activities can in itself be a reinforcer, depending somewhat on the individual circum-stances. (What my mom told me about boys is also true about dogs—leave 'em wanting more!)

Prompts—Lend a Helping Hand...But Then Make Them Stand On Their Own Four Feet

Prompts are events that help initiate a response or events that help elicit a behaviour. They are big aids in manufacturing behaviour and also in bringing the dog to an understanding of the cue. Prompts are antecedent events— some of the stuff that happens before a behaviour. They can be predictors of R+ or aversives. In most cases, particularly for our competition dogs, the ultimate goal is to be able to get the terminal response, or end behaviour, without the use of prompts. This is where **fading** comes in. Fading is the process of getting rid of all of the special conditions and helper prompts, thus paring the cue down to the bare bones of what you want the dog to respond to.

The syntax for using prompts to change the cue that elicits the behaviour is as follows:

1) New cue

2) Slight pause (count to 1)

3) Old cue or prompt

4) Behaviour

5) Consequences.

When you have done this several times, the dog begins to associate the new cue with the old cue or prompt. In anticipation, the dog will begin to perform the behaviour on the new cue. In order for that to happen, you must fade out the prompt. First, give the new cue. Now instead of a slight pause of 1, count to 5 or 10. Be patient. See what the dog offers. If indeed the association between the new cue and prompt or old cue has been made, the dog will react with the desired behaviour. If the dog offers the incorrect behaviour, use an NRM and begin a new trial, going back to using the prompt after a slight pause of 1 count for another 10 to 20 repetitions. Then try again with the long pause. When the dog offers the correct behaviour in absence of the prompt—Celebrate!

Chaining: Behaviour Sequences or Workin' on The Chain Gang...

Chaining is the process of stringing a whole bunch of individual behaviours into one sequence of responses. In most technical literature, chaining

Chaining is the process of stringing a number of behaviours into one sequence of responses.

Next, the handler guides the dog over the jump.

When the dog completes the jump successfully, he is rewarded.

means, specifically, **backtraining.** Backtraining is a useful concept when building a behaviour sequence. The first requirement is that you have taught all of the individual components (each link) of the chain first. Then a long complicated behaviour chain is taught backward—that's right, you teach the last behaviour in the chain first. Then you add the second-to-last and so on until you are at the beginning of the long behaviour series. An example: In teaching the high jump, the terminal response (end result, finished behaviour) begins with a dog that sits at your side in heel position. The exercise then progresses as follows: You give a stay command and signal, you throw the dumbbell, you command "Take," the dog leaves your side, jumps the jump, scoops up the dumbbell, returns over the jump, sits in front of you, presents the dumbbell, you command "Thank you," the dog gives you the dumbbell, you command "Swing," and the dog returns to heel position. Exercise finished. Wow! Simple to watch, complicated to teach. And just think how the dog feels! Let's assume that the dog already knows the components of the exercise: retrieving, recall, jumping, fronts with the dumbbell, and finishes, and you have done lots of motivational retrieves over the high jump. Now you can begin to chain the formal exercise. Begin with the dog in a sit/stay, holding the dumbbell on the other side of the jump. Do a recall over the high jump. When this is solid, you can add the first part of the exercise, the sitting by you at heel. This way the dog is going from an unknown portion of the exercise into the known part of the exercise. Therefore, from Spot's point of view, the work gets easier rather than more difficult as you progress into the exercise.

As you go on to more and more complex behaviours, like the long behaviour sequences we encounter in competitive obedience, you must make sure that you unpredictably (variable ratio, variable interval) reinforce each link of the chain. Keep in mind that chains break at their weakest link, so you want all of those links to have a strong reinforcement history. Common in behaviour sequences is that the middle behaviours or beginning behaviours begin to break down, because people tend to apply R+ in a predictable manner at the "end" of the behaviour sequence. To keep the exercises fresh and reinforcing, I do the exercises out of order. I break off in the middle of a chain and play a game. Boredom is a big "de-motivator" for all of us! Use your imagination. One of my favorite things about reinforcement training is that if my timing is off, the worst my dog gets out of it is a free cookie not an unfair punishment. I'll take that!

Summary for Chaining and Other Important Stuff You Really Need to Remember

- Reinforce the things you see your dog doing right.
- Concentrate your energy on telling the dog he's right.
- The real "T" word in training is not treat, it's timing.
- Make use of opportunity training (talk about little effort on the trainer's part). This is a boon for lazy trainers (like me).
- Set Spot up for success (and you, too).
- To be an R+, whatever you are offering has to be something the dog likes, such as food, games, touch, etc. Compile a list of things your dog likes. Now don't leave it buried on your desk or in a dusty corner of your mind. Use it!
- An RM buys time, provides information, and gets you away from relying so heavily on a primary R+ (like food). Your special word/sound serves as a memory marker for the dog.
- Take a "picture" of the behaviour with your RM.
- A no reward mark (NRM) is valuable info. You can double the information you give the dog by using it.

- Use small steps to get there.
- Don't lose your cool.
- Practice your timing—you can do it!
- In technical literature, shaping proceeds forward; chaining proceeds backward. A whole bunch of individual behaviors strung together is a behavior sequence. This is just FYI.

so, how do you help the dog pick out the pattern?

The lack of careful management, planning, and application of a reinforcement schedule is where many people go wrong in their training program. This is why they get disgusted and say things like, "That's a bunch of 'you know what.' Reinforcement training doesn't work. The dog just wants the food." (Like the dog *shouldn't* want the food—what is up with that? Like it is a big surprise that the dog wants the food?) You have probably heard of or seen the *Where's Waldo* books for children. They are a "find the hidden objects" sort of puzzle. The premise involves very detailed pictures with the object being to find Waldo, with the only constant (pattern) being Waldo's hat and glasses.

Dogs are trying to figure humans out without the benefit of human spoken language. They have to pick out "patterns" in the environment and try to match the reinforcement history to specific behaviours. All of this with humans no less, who tend to rely on the spoken word—which makes us very clumsy communicators from the dog's point of view. Dogs are subtle and sophisticated communicators if they are allowed to be, using mostly body language. Humans just need to be sensitive to the means that the dog uses to "talk" to us. With the usual inconsistent, sketchy, or nonexistent reinforcement history we provide for our pets, it becomes more of a surprise that any of them get trained at all!

Reinforcement schedules are what make the pattern discernible for the dog.

Reinforcement Schedules

The reinforcement schedules are fixed ratio, fixed interval, variable ratio, and variable interval. A brief description is as follows:

With **fixed interval**, an R+ is delivered reliably at a given time, like every 20 seconds or like your paycheck every Friday. With fixed ratio, the same amount of R+ is given for that behaviour on a predictable basis: 1 behaviour = 1 cookie. Think of vending machines.

With variable interval, the R+ is delivered at different times; you never know when it's coming. With variable ratio, the R+ is delivered in variable (different and unpredictable) quantities. The common analogy here is a slot machine.

The following describes each reinforcement schedule in more detail.

A **fixed schedule** means the same number or amount of behaviours predictably yields the same amount and timing of

When teaching your dog a new behaviour, she will learn more quickly if you provide consistent feedback on a fixed reinforcement schedule.

the reinforcer. It is interesting to note that leaving a behaviour on a fixed schedule infinitely may cause the behaviour to fade or disappear. So when do you use this kind of reinforcement schedule? I use it in the learning phase when the dog is still unsure of the antecedent-to-behaviour connection. I will also use a lure fairly predictably to elicit certain behaviours. In short, use the fixed schedule long enough for the pupil to make the connection between the antecedent and the behaviour. This is the learning stage in which your dog learns two things: 1) his behaviour has discernable consequences, and 2) there is an event, context, or signal that "cues" him. During the learning stage:

1 behaviour = 1 reinforcement
or fixed ratio (FR).

What you are doing is building up a **reinforcement history**. The stronger the reinforcement history, the stronger the behaviour will resist deterioration. Keep in mind the natural inclinations of your animal. Even though I have a fairly strong reinforcement history for a recall, calling one of my terriers off a rat before it is dead will be pretty questionable. I understand that they are bred to hunt vermin. In fact, I do keep my barn clear of vermin by allowing them to hunt and kill rats. Of course, this practice means my terriers have a reinforcement history that is in line with their instincts. In this area I wisely practice behaviour management. If in doubt, my terriers are on leash so I can keep them out of trouble.

You can compare a reinforcement history in training to beginning a savings account. For a long time, you put money in the bank every week. Then after a bit, it adds up and that money begins to pay you back in interest. Up front, you put a lot of time and effort into training, but the interest paid back to you by having such a good friend is well worth the investment. And dog training is not subject to inflation. What an advantage! Guaranteed return on your effort, and it's not subject to the whims of Wall Street. It just doesn't get any better than that.

Now, we go on to the advanced stuff. As quickly as possible, move a behavior on to a **variable schedule** of reinforcement. That is, the best efforts get one, two, or more cookies. Fantastic efforts may get a special reinforcer that I don't use often, like cheese or a game—a special reward mark to aid the dog's memory. As soon as I see the animal getting the connections straight, I will ask for two, three, or even five behaviours for one reinforcement. I always give verbal praise lavishly, but those primary reinforcers get more difficult to get as I gradually raise the criteria. If I am working on several behaviours, each in varying stages of completion, the new behaviours get lots of reinforcement and the maintenance behaviours get less. The dog will tell you where you need to reinforce.

For example, if my dog is trained for the Novice Recall and he is breaking the stay portion of the exercise, where does the dog need R+ applied? Well, take a guess—I need to R+ the stay more. (Note: The

When you are working with your dog, you are working with inherited behaviours. Some behaviours are naturally reinforcing for your dog.

Novice Recall exercise consists of placing your dog in a sit/stay, walking approximately 20 steps, turning to face the dog, and then on the judge's command calling your dog to a front position. Many dogs are eager to get to the handler and so break the stay before they are called.)

In this situation specifically, I will take two or three steps to leave the dog after my stay command and then back up and deliver a primary reinforcer (cookie). I will go all the way to the end of the ring, turn, assume a formal position, and then return to the dog and deliver a cookie or release him to eat a treat that I toss. I will then do the whole exercise, including the recall portion and the front. Sometimes I will begin a game with the dog for a good stay. Yup, I go part of the way, turn around, and begin a game. I don't do these in any particular order; in fact, it is a very good idea to mix it all up so that the dog has to pay close attention. I mean, from the dog's point of view, you just never know what that handler will do—he is so interesting. The point being that if part of a behaviour sequence is deteriorating, the dog is telling you something. Pay attention.

Part of being variable means using different kinds of food. Again, from the dog's point of view, "I might get another piece of kibble, but I just *might* get cheese." Part of being variable also means mixing up the exercises—don't run

Vary your training routine by taking occasional play breaks to keep things fun and interesting.

through the same old stuff in the same old order time after time after time. Yawn—Goodness, one gets bored just reading about it.

Variable means being unpredictable. Got good heel work? Throw up your hands, scream like a banshee, and have a party. Not all the time, of course. Sometimes, use just an RM, a favorite toy to initiate a game, or "freeze" and deliver an RM and a cookie. Be unpredictable, remember?

In summary, mastery of variable reinforcement schedules means you will be an extremely successful trainer. You will, in fact, be in the top echelon of elite trainers.

Specific Ways to Be Variable

- Stop and play a game. Yes, you can give yourself permission to play a game right in the middle of your training session. It's great, just like ordering dessert first!

- Use different kinds of food. Sometimes all it takes for the animal to decide to put out a little extra effort and continue to try is to up the ante—use better food. Once the dog is performing the exercise well, you don't have to use the better food. The dog will, in fact work for no food on occasion once he is transferred to a variable schedule.

- Deliver your PR (primary reinforcer/cookie) in different ways. Sometimes I hand it to the dog with my left hand. Sometimes I toss it on the floor and release Spot to get it. Sometimes I throw the food over my head with my right hand to the dog, while he's sitting in heel position. Sometimes I spit food that was stored in my mouth at the dog—occasionally, he even catches it. Sometimes I deliver several cookies in a row, feeding one from the right hand, one from the left hand, one from the right hand, etc. You get the picture.

- Mix up the exercises. Break off exercises in the middle or do a complete run-through sometimes.

- Train some sessions with lots of food, train some sessions with no food, train some sessions with just play; mix them all up—be variable.

What You Need To Remember About Schedules

- Use a fixed schedule until Spot establishes the trend between the antecedent (cue) and the behaviour.

- Use a variable (specifically: variable interval, variable ratio, and intermittent with reinforcement variety) schedule to maintain behaviour.

- Spot will tell you where you need to apply more R+ to keep behaviours in their top form.

You Don't Get a Second Chance
to Make a First Impression

The first time a dog attempts a behaviour—any behaviour, desirable or undesirable—is very memorable for them. Make first attempts at obedience exercises pleasant, fun, and relaxed. Give the dog a good first impression about those behaviours you wish to see again in the future. For those behaviours you wish never to see again as long as you live, nip them in the bud. If the first time a dog attempts to get on the table is met with an appropriate punisher that results in having no fun, he will not resort to this behaviour very many times. (An appropriate punisher should be humane and appropriate for that individual.) In other words, if you can be absolutely consistent in spoiling the fun in the situation, the behaviour will extinguish pretty quickly. In short, the behaviour didn't pay off, and dogs don't do what doesn't pay off. Back that up with lots of social approval and goodies for not engaging in unwanted behaviours. Apply R+ to the absence of unwanted behaviours; the R+ portion of this protocol is more important than the punishing consequence. If presented properly, the consequence makes the scenario very clear for the dog and makes the right road easy to choose.

Taking advantage of this rule is the best way to deter your dog from undesirable behaviour. If you can prevent or catch a first incident (like getting on the counter) before the behaviour gets a big reinforcement history going, your chances of the behaviour approaching extinction quickly become quite excellent. Once you are fighting that prior reinforcement history (Spot got to eat a bite a the roast on the kitchen counter before you could intervene), the process of getting rid of the unwanted behaviour is a little tougher going.

Do the same for those events that you wish your dog to

First events are big memory markers. Make sure you teach you puppy the correct behaviour from the very beginning.

Positive Reinforcement

remember favorably. For example, his first trip to the vet. Take Spot in, have all the techs and the vet feed Spot yummy cookies, and then take Spot home. Many Schutzhund trainers introduce their dogs to the training field by taking them to the location and engaging the dog in play—with the trainer only. This teaches the young student that training is fun, fun, and more fun. Only after that concept is firmly implanted, does the trainer begin the serious work. That first impression carries the dog through competition exercises, and he brings that joy into his work.

First events are big memory markers. Make sure that the dog is remembering what you want him to have remembered.

ready, set, go...

Now you have all of the tools that you need to teach a behaviour to your pet, your brother, your sister, or your spouse! (Note: You may discover that humans do not find spitting food at them to be reinforcing, but it does work great with dogs.) Is this exciting or what!?

A Recipe For Success

To train successfully, you need the following ingredients:

Planning for the ABCs

- A signal (antecedent)
- The big picture goal (terminal response behaviour)
- Today's goal (target behaviour)
- Timing
- Primary reinforcer (consequence)
- Reward mark (consequence)
- No reward mark (consequence)
- Willingness to be flexible
- Judgement
- Pupil
- Notebook to record progress

Don't look at this list and think,"Oh my! That's way too much!" Hogwash. This is so much easier than you think. Stick with me and I'll tell you a secret!

Pssst! ...Some Secrets About How to Identify R+
for Your Pupil

- An event/food may be reinforcing for one dog, but not for another.
- An event/food may have a reinforcing effect for one dog under some circumstances or at some times, but not under other circumstances or at other times. If the situation is new/distracting, up the ante. Using different or better food may change the dog's mind about doing this behaviour under these circumstances. Then you at least get the ball rolling, and the dog begins to generalize the behaviour. Soon the behaviour is under stimulus control in the new situation.

Open the Door to Behaviour: Keys to R+

- High frequency. That means be generous.
- Short latency between behaviour and consequence. That means good timing. Nail that behaviour with an RM and a primary (food). Now!
- Unpredictability. (Unpredictable things are exciting and grab your attention. Bored mammals are un-motivated mammals.)
- Do things differently. (Use lots of different R+—different food, different games, change the order of your exercises. Don't practice the same stuff all

A reward may be reinforcing for one dog, but may not work for another. There will be times when you need to increase or change the reinforcer to get the desired behaviour. Unpredictability is a vital part of variable reinforcement.

Dogs are just like humans in that they need clear and accurate information to avoid becoming frustrated. Frustration will result in stress and can slow down learning.

the time. Be fun! Have fun!)

- Use an RM and an NRM. The biggie! Dogs get to be information junkies just like we do. They love having accurate information and dislike being confused and frustrated. So be clear and concise in your communications.

training to teach a specific task

The first step to teaching a task or lesson is to have a reward mark (RM) for the subject. (A quick recap: For dogs, I get about 40 tiny little goodies about one-half the size of a fingernail. Then I make the sound of the conditioned reinforcer or reward mark and deliver the treat).

Begin the training session in a nondistracting environment for the first few trials. In this exercise, my goal is to have the dog sit immediately when I tell him to and to stay there until I release him. To teach a dog that does not know how to sit, I would go about the exercise as follows.

You can wait for the behaviour to occur naturally if you wish (opportunity training), but for the impatient among us, you can manufacture the behaviour. I begin with a food lure. This does two things: Attracts the dog to me (it's hard to get any behaviours to reinforce if the dog is running away from me) and gives me a way to communicate to the dog the position I want him to have.

I call the dog to me or wait for him to approach. I R+ the approach so it will happen again. (In this case, I feed the approach until a good reinforcement history for approach is established.) Soon, being next to you is strongly associated with opportunities to earn R+, and you will find that previously elusive canine right there under your nose. (If you are working with a very distractable individual, stand on the four- or six-foot leash so your dog cannot wander far enough to engage in reinforcing activities that do not involve you.) Now that I have his attention, I hold the food in front of his nose and raise it over his head and toward his tail. If you hold your hand in the right place, as he looks up to keep track of the food, his bottom will hit the ground. The moment the dog's bottom hits the

By using food, you can elicit certain behaviours from your dog. For example, when you raise a food treat above your dog's head, he will automatically sit. If you mark and reinforce the behaviour, he will perform it again.

ground, relinquish the food. If you have trained the animal to a reward mark, you can "click" or say your special word, "Good" or "Yes," then relinquish the food. When I am teaching classes, my constant chant to my students is "Mark it and feed it!" It works with them, so I will use it with you also.

Please notice the absence of moving lips and chatting at the dog in the above scenario. Be quiet! If you are learning new software on the computer, do you want someone saying your name and talking to you? Stay quiet so the dog can concentrate. Give him only the information he needs. The technical reason is this: If you know that dogs assimilate behaviours principally through associative learning and the dog is standing, sniffing, or looking around while you are reciting "Sit, sit, sit, sit" like a mantra, what behaviour do you think your dog is associating your antecedent with? (Associative learning has to do with the experience of pairing or associating a behaviour with whatever event is happening right now and in the same time frame immediately preceding, during, or following said behaviour.) In teaching the dog to sit, we have just successfully **manufactured** a behaviour using shaping. (Baby steps, baby steps. Spot will be doing a sit/stay before you know it!)

Not until you can elicit the behaviour predictably or can manufacture the behaviour predictably, do you add the cue. You need to *have* the behaviour in order to connect a cue to it, so that the animal does not become needlessly confused. Because of associative learning, you cannot name a behaviour that does not yet exist in this dog's repertoire. In this instance, I already have a hand signal of sorts (raising my hand over the dog's head), but I may want to add a verbal command. This is the place. Just before the dog sits (watch for that intention behaviour), say "Sit"—just once. This helps the dog associate the behaviour of sitting with the verbal cue of "Sit."

At that point, when you give your cue to sit and the dog begins to assume the sit position, he is beginning to understand and associate the behaviour you want—sitting—with the cue you have chosen to use to get the behaviour—a verbal, "Sit."

We have just successfully **shaped** a behaviour and **put it on cue**.

When you practice this, you are still on a fixed reinforcement schedule (FR1), so the dog can pick out the pattern.

Operant conditioning not only allows your dog to participate in training to the fullest extent possible, it also allows his personality to shine through.

The next step is to move on to a variable schedule to maintain the behaviour. It is time to do this once the animal has not made a mistake 8 out of 10 times, or 80 out of 100 times, or to express this concept in percentages, an 80-percent correct ratio. (An 80-percent correct ratio is considered learning for humans—*ABC's of Behaviour Shaping,* audio tape by Ted Turner.) At this juncture, it is safe to assume that the animal is beginning to connect the antecedent "Sit" with a certain position. The individual and the behaviour determine how many repetitions will be required to reach this stage. For some animals, you are literally talking about eight repetitions, for others you are talking many more. When you begin to see this 80-percent correct ratio, you can be sure that the connection has been made and the pattern established—you have lift off! Now the behaviour is ready to be transferred to a variable or maintenance schedule. This is that important place in time when the primary reinforcer gets more difficult to earn. As you vary the reinforcement schedule, you will initially see some variation in the behaviour as well. For lesser efforts—lesser pay; for the better efforts—better pay. In short, be unpredictable, give verbal praise only sometimes, an RM paired with food sometimes, toss a toy sometimes—you get the idea. When you get an extremely desirable response from Spot, provide extra nice R+, like maybe five cookies instead of one cookie. Spot gets something every time—he just doesn't know which something it might be. We all love surprises!

If I encounter an error on the dog's part in the learning stage, I provide lots of help and tolerance and use the NRM, which means "Give me some other behaviour because that wasn't it and you won't get any cookies from me!" For those instances when the dog is *choosing* NOT to do the behaviour, use a correction. How do you tell? Choosing not to do the behaviour is blatant and willfull disobedience. This is a very different scenario from "Spot is trying, but he is unsure of what you want." If you saw a person teaching a child to write, and the child did not know how to make a certain letter, would you punish the child?

I would certainly hope not! I should like to think that all of us would offer help in the form of teaching. Most instances of what many people call disobedience—out of spite, revenge, or bad attitude—are actually learning problems and not blatant and willful disobedience. I, personally, give the dog the benefit of the doubt. Nobody gets up in the morning and tries to get it all wrong just so they can be miserable. Your dog doesn't either.

Now let's assume that you have truly done your homework and actually trained a behaviour. However, the dog is

If your dog makes a mistake with a well-known behaviour, do not lose your temper. Calmly use a reward mark and help your dog to succeed.

just being nonchalant about responding and still does not sit when you tell him to. At this juncture, you could give Spot a look at what happens if he *chooses* not to sit—physically guide the dog into the sit position (gently but not in a friendly way, more in a neutral way). This may be done with a gentle but steady lift of his collar. Very light pressure is used and the name of the game is outlasting the dog, not physically subduing him. **Big reminder: No jerking! No yelling! No repeating the cue!** Maintain this gentle, steady lift no matter what the dog does. If your dog throws a temper tantrum, remain calm, cool, and collected. Don't talk. Remain neutral. Maintain your position until Spot "gives in" and sits. As soon as Spot sits, immediately release the collar. (If you do not know the dog, or your dog has a history of aggression, do not even think about this! Confrontation is not what we are about here; what we are about is making the dog a bit uncomfortable, so the decision about sitting is easier to make next time.) Give verbal praise, social approval, and a treat only if this is the first time you've used this correction. After this first time, do not give food if a correction is required. Then begin another trial. As soon as Spot sits without help, have a party. This is how the dog figures out the pattern—by use of appropriate consequences, timing, and reinforcement schedules.

The dog has figured out the pattern by use of appropriate consequences, timing, and reinforcement schedules.

To obtain the stay portion of the exercise, you begin to raise the criteria. That means the steps get closer and closer to your terminal response or the end goal. In this scenario you begin to ask for longer sitting behaviours before you feed the behaviour. You are working on duration. My rule with stays is duration before distance. In this manner, I have trained my dogs to remain in a stay on one command for up to 45 minutes at a time. You can, of course, go longer if you wish, just shape the behaviour.

Realistically, you may find that you don't want to make the exercise more and more difficult all the time. My experience in training real dogs in the real world has been that I am more successful using the following type of technique. Let's say that my dog has the following known threshold—a 5-second sit/stay. The following session is an example of how to increase the threshold.

Trial #1—Obtain a Sit Provide the consequence after: 3 seconds	The consequence is: RM (thereby buying myself five more seconds with no food) Remind "Stay" (as a reminder—a landmark that "you are on the right road.")
5 seconds	RM & Primary—"Stay" Tip: I wait for the dog to gulp the treat, then he usually looks up at me—that's when I say, "Stay"
3 seconds	RM & Primary—"Stay"
7 seconds	RM
4 seconds	RM & Primary—"Stay"
8 seconds	RM & Primary — See if you need to repeat "Stay," look for intention behaviour of the dog beginning to break
3 seconds	RM—Release and Game
Begin Trial #2: Obtain Another Sit 10 seconds	The consequence is: RM & Primary

My dog just did 33 seconds with help and 10 seconds without help. So I just bumped my 5-second stay into the 10-second threshold in two trials. You make very fast progress this way. The dog is getting lots of R+ for staying and gaining confidence with every trial.

Depending on the dog, you may have to get the behaviour with a food lure or keep adding the hand signal prompt anywhere from 4 to 200 times before the animal understands the behaviour *and* associates the verbal cue of "Sit" with the behaviour and will perform reliably.

Remember, we always begin training a new behaviour in a safe area free from distractions. Dogs tend to "localize" learning. That is, if you teach the dog to sit in the kitchen, once you move into the living room you may have to start right back at the beginning. When you get the desired behaviour reliably in three or four locations, the procedure begins to happen more quickly each time. In some instances, you can then get the behaviour anywhere, anytime. Other behaviours will require more "road work." This process is called **generalizing**. Read on!

taking it on the road

The real goal of a training or behaviour modification program is to increase the chances of responsiveness to instructions. In other words, you are telling the dog: "Please do what I tell you to do—when I tell you to do it!" When a behaviour occurs much more often than not in the presence of a given learned cue or antecedent, it is said to be under stimulus control. I believe this is the stage we are all looking for.

Discrimination and **generalization** are how all of us mammal-types figure out how to behave in different situations. We take a look at the context of the situation, analyze past experiences and the instructions given, and then base our behaviour, to the best of our ability, on the information we have. Our dogs are no different. We're all just trying to figure out how to "find Waldo" (pick out the pattern). So work with your dog on this, rather than taking a confrontational position. The balance is difficult enough to achieve without infighting among the ranks.

Discrimination and generalization are opposite of each other. **Discrimination** has to do with responding differently to different situations. The environment, cue, or other antecedents may differ—either a little or a lot—and these differences elicit different behaviours. **Generalization** has to do with transferring a behaviour intact from one situation and into another, even if those situations are different.

Discrimination is what helps all of us to figure out what cue to respond to and helps us to pick out the pattern and discard extraneous information. Discrimination is the device by which different contingencies are made clear. This really means that Spot comes to understand which cue specifically belongs to which behaviour. The ability to make discriminations gives us information about "what is different and what is the same" in this context. A wild animal must make many of these discriminations and generalizations to survive. It is a wise gazelle that realizes alligators may lurk near the watering hole. The discrimination that the gazelle needs to make is to look for those signs that indicate an alligator is near and, if so, wait to get a drink. If the gazelle generalizes that all waterholes must be checked out, he will live to drink again. If he discriminates too closely—only this one waterhole has alligators—the gazelle could make a fatal discrimination. I

A well-trained dog will behave in the same manner in any situation. Punch knows that "sit" means "sit," no matter where she happens to be.

hate it when gazelles do this on TV, but it does seem to make the alligators happy.

The moral of this tale actually has nothing to do with gazelles. The point is that you must make the effort to ensure that behaviours will transfer from one situation into another. Dogs are extremely specific learners. Did Spot learn to sit in the living room? Chances are "Sit" must also be re-taught in the kitchen and again in the front yard and again on the sidewalk. We used to joke at the barn about some of the horses we were training—"If you stop for lunch, you'll have to retrain her!" What we were referring to, of course, were those animals that didn't seem to be able to generalize *any* behaviours. (I have also encountered some coworkers in various jobs with the same trait. Just keep telling yourself through gritted teeth that "She just doesn't generalize well.") Everyone has trouble generalizing some behaviours. For instance, if a child touches a hot stove and then comes to the conclusion that all stoves are very dangerous and refuses to even be in the same room with a stove—well, that child will be an extremely hungry adult. That is a dangerous generalization. If the child makes the connection that you don't touch the surface of stoves with your bare hand, because stoves may be hot—that is a more useful generalization. In my van, you push a rectangular-shaped rocker button down to put the windows up. I hopped into my friend's car the other day and did the same movement. Nothing happened. She has some weird button in her car you sort of lift up to open the window. I had generalized my "window-shutting" behaviour. I had to learn a new discrimination to work the windows in her car.

Those who discriminate too closely must learn each lesson over and over in each new situation. So it is clear that a balance between generalization and discrimination must be achieved. My experience is that discrimination/ generalization balances vary greatly from breed to breed and also among individuals in a breed. But overall, if you look at those breeds that people perceive as being "easy to train," what you really see are those animals that make vast generalizations quickly. To obtain a consistent response, my Fox Terrorists take many more repetitions in many more locations than my German Shepherd Dog. Though I haven't figured it out mathematically (there would be some interesting statistics), it is definitely not my imagination. Breanna, Punch, and Dervish—my dogs—and the many rescue Smooths I have worked with just don't come under stimulus control well. And it is not that the Terriers are "more alert" than the German Shepherds. However, one thing that Fox Terriers do is process discriminations and generalizations differently than German Shepherds. Obviously, there are more factors at work than just the ability to generalize, but I see generalization as being one of the main reasons.

Karen Pryor, a marine mammal trainer and pioneer in animal training methodology, calls lack of generalization the "new tank syndrome." When working with marine mammals, she discovered (and better yet, wrote down for all of us) that when trained dolphins were moved from the tank they had been trained in to a new tank, the animals temporarily forgot everything that had been under stimulus control in the old tank. Once the dolphins were in their new environment and had assured themselves that they were safe, they were comfortable enough to resume their behaviours. A quick review, beginning with easy steps (otherwise known as going back to kindergarten), brings your pupil back into the prior behaviour "Ph.D.-level" category rapidly.

Let me ask you this: When you walk into a cocktail party, or any other new location that you are not familiar with, do you move into the room staring piercingly at the person you enter the room with, with absolutely no other thoughts on your mind? (If so, it must be new love, and it's very likely that it will wear off...) I don't. I immediately assess the situation, look all around me, catalogue where the food and beverages are, see who is present—anybody I know?—and spot where the restroom might be, along with deciding whether or not I like the wallpaper. This is an instinctive reaction and hales from primal times. When you enter a new area, your first instinct is to figure out: "Am I safe? Where am I?" I don't see my dog doing anything different—except to him the sidewalk in front of the house is a cocktail party.

In short, just don't expect the dog to perform behaviours in all situations, even behaviours he knows in another setting, without some concerted effort on your part to show the dog that "Sit" means sit—in the living room, in the dining room, in the backyard, in the front yard, at dog class, and in the show ring.

Different situations can provide different distractions. If your dog seems to forget his training in a new environment, go back to the beginning and reinforce what you have taught him.

Rules for Generalizing Behaviour

- The same dog will discriminate and/or generalize different exercises at different rates of learning.
- If the dog needs help, go back to kindergarten temporarily. Review the steps you used to get the finished behaviour. You will be able to move pretty quickly, because the dog already has some idea about what you might want.
- I take baby behaviours on the road. I initially teach the new behaviour in nondistracting environments. I can elicit the behaviour while still giving some help to Spot.

Big Note: Fears tend to generalize way out of proportion to the actual context, and then they become phobias. Fear will always override every other emotion. In a fearful animal, very little, if any learning is taking place. He is merely reacting to his environment. (I suggest you read *On Talking Terms With Dogs: Calming Signals,* by Turid Rugaas, published by Legacy by Mail, Inc., 1997. Terry Ryan also has written material about this subject. You need to understand what stress looks like and how to teach the dog coping mechanisms to deal with stress.)

It is interesting to note that fear and undertraining can look similar in our dogs. The dog in the obedience ring that is still confused about an exercise may display the same sort of body language that a fearful dog would. Confusion and fear can be related in the dog's mind for many reasons, some of them learned. To clarify: The factor exists that confusion and indecision about what to do in a given context make the dog feel uneasy enough to display fearful body language. The other possibility is that the dog has been punished in the past for confusion (probably by a trainer who really didn't know how to tell the difference between "I'm trying" and "I'm not trying"), therefore linking confusion and punishment to the behaviour, resulting in the fearful body language.

What do you do when your dog starts to display the stress of "not knowing" or being intimidated? In this instance, help your dog to succeed with some "easy" behaviors that he enjoys doing, and then begin to raise the criteria when the dog displays a little more confidence. This will teach the dog that he can cope and overcome his stress to have some fun. Sometimes gaining a sight distance from the chaos and returning to the scene helps.

In summary, go back to kindergarten, help your dog succeed and keep placing him in new situations so that he learns to cope effectively and leave his fears behind.

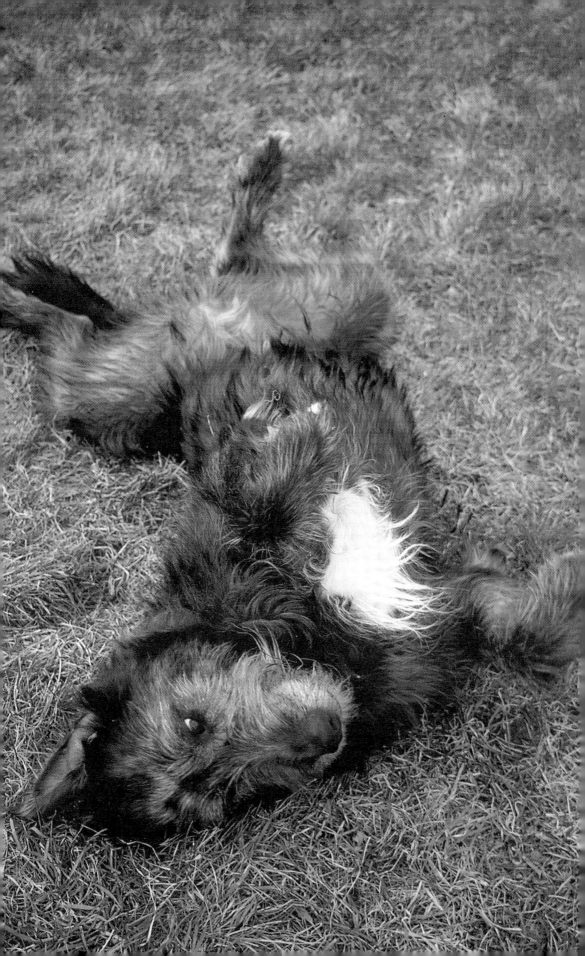

i can't get no satisfaction...

Why doesn't my dog perform all behaviours equally in all locations once I've taught the behaviour? Am I a bad trainer or is the dog a moron? Are there possibly some training secrets that I don't know about?

Because we feel such kinship to our dogs and they are, like us, a social species, many people think that dogs learn right and wrong. This gives moral overtones to behaviour and muddies the waters of dog training in a big way. Forget all that. What dogs do quickly pick up on is safe versus dangerous. Please dispel "The Lassie Myth" from your training! And just think how liberating it is for both you and the dog when you don't project all this personal stuff (you might call it emotional baggage, and I can bring many other less complimentary comments to mind) into your training sessions and into daily life. So leave your personal baggage in the closet or somewhere else when you train. The exercise in self-control will be good for you.

Stuff You Encounter Training Dogs in the Real World

If you get nonconformity or outright mutiny to a request for behaviour, there is a reason for it. Humans don't just wander around doing stuff at random and neither do dogs. Dogs would not have survived and been madly successful as a species if they did. So when you do not get compliance, you need to look further for the reason. Don't get angry and frustrated, or if you do, get over it. Put your dog in his crate, figure out *why* you're having the problem, and fix it.

There is a chasm between the behaviour you have and the behaviour you want from your dog. Training is the bridge you build across the chasm.

Undertraining or Lost in the Wilderness

To have a trained animal, you have to be unafraid in the wilderness. The repetitions required to have excellent response in almost any situation shall be numbered many as the trees in a forest. If you are unwilling to take the time to build the bridge, you are going to stay right where you are. So, "Play it again, Sam!" Good trainers are willing to put in the vast quantity of repetitions that will be necessary to train the behaviour. Good trainers can tolerate the boredom that comes with the many repetitions and keep the dog interested in the process. For those of you who have a low boredom tolerance, do what I do: Train in small bursts. If I do 2 or 3 trials of a behaviour every day for 10 days, I've got 30 trials in. If I can do those 3 trials twice a day for 10 days, I have 60 trials in just 10 days. Good athletes know the same secret—it really is just like the tennis shoe ad says: "Just do it!" Doing those trials, in most cases, takes very little time. I can do 3 sit or down trials in 2 to 3 minutes. I can even do 3 retrieve trials in 5 minutes. It really comes down to just taking the time to do it.

Don't blame Spot because he isn't trained, because quite frankly my dear, he doesn't give a damn. Dogs are perfectly happy being the lovely, complete little beings that they are. If properly trained, dogs become equally content to follow the rules. As a matter of fact, structure alone, properly presented, can prevent a myriad of problem-type behaviours from developing.

People tend to see a few correct responses and assume that the puppy has it down pat. Trust me, he doesn't. The optimism displayed in this circumstance is touching, but unrealistic. You need many reps in many locations before your dog really understands what you want. For behaviours that aren't in line with the dog's natural tendencies, you are talking an even longer row to hoe. So start hoeing. Five repetitions a day translates into 35 repetitions in 7 days, or 70 reps if you do them twice a day. In no time, you are there. Think of the mental muscle you and your puppy will develop.

If you get a non-response to a cue, ask yourself this question: How many trials have I really done? My friend, Mary, and I keep each other honest when training. On many occasions, we have been training together and inevitably receive a non-response to what we think should be a well-known cue. One or the other of us will wail: "(S)he knows this! I started teaching this *months* ago!" And the other replies, "But how many actual trials of this behaviour have you done?" More often than not, even though the behaviour was started six months ago, we count up the actual training sessions that we worked on that particular behaviour and discover that the dog may have done the behaviour a whopping total of ten times—not enough. So don't look *only* at the time frame, think about how many actual repetitions of the behaviour have been performed. Yet another good reason to keep a notebook or count on a friend with a dog-training-oriented photographic memory. (It is a known phenomenon that even if you have photographic memory for dog training, it may not work with your own dog. You might need someone else to give you perspective.) Bottom line—If you want the behaviour, you have to do the repetitions.

Incorrect Responses—Why is This Happening to Me?

Experienced trainers *expect* a high occurrence of "wrong" responses. When you see an incorrect response, you have a golden opportunity to provide the dog with feedback about the behaviour, for instance, an NRM, elicit the correct behaviour, and then R+ that. The feedback will give the dog information about which road to take in the future. Your notebook will show you that over time, the big picture will show a gradual rise in correct trials.

If a dog is in doubt about the requested behaviour, he usually resorts to:
• the most recently reinforced behaviour;
• a behaviour with the most extensive reinforcement history;
• a more intense version of the behaviour being shaped;
• the first behaviour learned;
• nothing.

This is known as the "training W," sometimes called the "pre-learning dip." Just about the time the trainer is feeling like he is home free with establishing the behaviour, the dog begins offering some other behaviour or stands around staring into space. When prompted, Spot looks at you like the cue word you have been using is completely foreign to him. What is likely happening is that Spot is making sure that the target behaviour is in fact what he is receiving R+ for. What looks like random behaviour to us is just an experiment to clarify the situation. Wait it out, provide appropriate feedback, and don't lose your cool. If the dog can handle it, I don't even offer much assistance; I let him figure it out. Dogs can do their own homework! Soon it occurs to Spot to offer the behaviour that he has been most recently reinforced for again, and you are now back in business. If he gets really befuddled, I will begin another trial, and this time use a helper prompt to get the dog started toward working in the right direction.

That second dip in the "W" often looks very similar to the first one, but may be even more intense. Many dogs get very frustrated at this point and act as if they expect you to give them some free R+. Work through this just like you did the last one, unless you are working with an aggressive dog.

Just FYI: If any aggression occurs due to delayed R+, you need to get the advice of an experienced pet behaviourist. I have worked with animals that do respond to punishment with aggression, and believe me when I tell you that to the inexperienced or very dominating animal, delayed R+ *is* an event that can be perceived by the animal as an aversive. It is one of the least confrontational methods you can choose, certainly, and I utilize it a lot when training stays and many other behaviours. Often, by delaying the R+, you really make headway, and you need to teach the animal about delayed R+ to get on any kind of maintenance reinforcement schedule. But if you see aggression, you need to get help! By aggression I mean behaviours like mounting, growling, hard eye contact, stiff legged or circling posturing, or sudden stillness with a slightly lowered head posture while staring at you or snapping at you. By the way, if you see this behaviour merely for delaying R+, I would *really* discourage you from attempting a collar correction.

You will not always see the learning "W" dramatically. I have trained many behaviours where it was almost not evident at all. If you have your reinforcement schedule well in hand, it is my opinion that you will see a smoother transition into understanding. On the other hand, if you do see the learning "W" up close and personal, don't get upset. This, too, shall pass. Exert some patience and hang in there with your criteria. Don't feel like a failure for backing up a couple of steps if you need to. I go backward and move forward in training many times for each behaviour. The trainer must be willing to be flexible. If you are having a bad day, don't despair. You and your faithful sidekick will soon have a stupendously successful day.

Learning Curves and Reinforcement Schedules

Inappropriate reinforcement schedules sabotage behaviours. If Spot is moved to a variable schedule before he has had a chance to pick out the pattern of A-B-C, you are shooting yourself in the foot. Spot will not function on too thin a schedule at the level of behaviour you want. A **thin schedule** refers to the least amount of reinforcement that you can get Spot to work for, while still maintaining the behaviour at the desired level of performance.

I confess this whole thin schedule thing caused me a lot of anguish. I kept reading everywhere that the behaviour itself would become reinforcing so that eventually you wouldn't need the food anymore. I also heard from dog trainers, both in person and in books, that Spot "should work for you because he loves you." Some of them frowned upon using food at all. On and on *ad nauseum*. Well kids, this is my personal experience: Some behaviours *will* maintain themselves; some behaviours will never get on a thin schedule. Guess what—you don't make those decisions; the pupil does. Much depends on the individual dynamics, the setting events, and what you want from your dog.

For Breanna, my oldest Fox Terrorist, very darned little ever stays on a very thin schedule for long when it comes to obedience behaviours. She has an extremely independent personality and is also the alpha Bitch (please note the capital "B") in my little dog pack. Her only true interest in life is being driven by her instinct to hunt vermin. Doing competition obedience with her has certainly been an interesting endeavor. This dog has trained me to be exceptionally grateful for every small crumb of her attention, because she has also shown me what lack of attention can look like, which would be the view of her backside rapidly disappearing into the distance. Traditional (correction-based) dog training was an absolute failure with this animal—her attitude quickly became "I don't know what you want, and now I don't care what you want." As a novice trainer, my timing left something to be desired as well. I was given two choices: A dull, dead performance that looked like the dog was forced to do it, or nothing at all. R+ turned this dog around. Now she is a joyful worker, happy, and animated. She puts her own twist of personality into each exercise. She prances when she heels, and when she finishes she leaps high into the air. On the signal exercise from a down, she leaps about 18 inches into the air and lands in a sit. However, I am still molding the clay I was given. And that means that if she smells a rat, obedience quickly takes a back seat. (I am not using "rat" as a figure of speech—I mean a real rat smell. Unfortunately for me, vermin live in many places, including the kinds of fairgrounds or other buildings in which you might hold an obedience trial. Being a terrier, she is also incredibly nosy and considers everything her business.) Breanna is extremely easy to distract. She discriminates very quickly, but generalizes very little. That can be translated into: She picks up on the gist of the exercise very quickly—but if anything changes, even the tiniest little detail, she is thrown for a loop by it and back to kindergarten we go. The good thing about Breanna is that she makes every other dog I work with look easy by comparison.

Maeve, my German Shepherd bitch, is as opposite from Breanna as you can possibly be. I obtained her as an 18-month-old adolescent with many behaviour issues. She not only discriminates quickly, she generalizes quickly. On top of that, she follows me all around asking, "What do you want now? What do you want now?" She can be placed on a thin schedule very quickly. She's a bit scary to train; it is very easy to be sloppy while training her because she is so forgiving.

What does the learning laboratory have to say about thin schedules? I was quite gratified to read that with maze-running rats in a controlled (nondistracting) environment, the ratio of primary reinforcement (food) needed to be 75 percent in order to maintain optimum levels of speed and accuracy (though I wish I would have found this out much sooner, because it could have saved me vast quantities of mental torment). That tidbit made me feel a lot better about the schedules I was using to maintain behaviour. Our dogs probably don't need 75 percent primary reinforcement (food), because we are using lots of other reinforcers, such as reward marks, access to toys, games, social approval, etc.

How can you tell if your R+ schedule is too thin? Spot will tell you. Where is the behaviour crumbling? That is the behaviour that needs "shoring up" with some extra R+. If you are already providing praise, you may have to up the ante and provide treats. If you are providing treats, you may need to up the ante and provide a special treat. You won't have to do this all the time, but occasionally you may need to. Don't get all upset about it. As long as you are getting what you want and the dog is getting what he wants, what is the problem? Semantics? I find that even if Spot knows the behaviour well in some contexts, or if the context or location differs dramatically, he will probably need some help with the first trial or two to get back on track in this new situation.

In summary:

- Undertraining is the first and foremost reason you don't get what you want.
- Don't presume learning.
- Be unafraid in the wilderness—expect to do a tremendous amount of trials and repetition.
- If the trainer becomes bored and boring, don't blame Spot. Be variable and unpredictable.
- Expect incorrect responses—they are an opportunity to provide appropriate feedback.
- Be tenacious. Non-response may be due to the fact that you are at the fifth trial of the 500 required to teach this exercise.
- Use an appropriate reinforcement schedule; fixed until the dog picks out the pattern, variable for maintenance of behaviour.
- If you see a dramatic "W" for a learning curve, don't be surprised. Feel good about it; it means that your dog is truly beginning to understand the scope of the requested behaviour.

Inadequate Timing
(or If You Don't Always Get What You Want...)

We have discussed this item at some length already. If the key principle in selling real estate is location, location, location, the key ingredient in dog training

When training your dog, the correct timing between the behaviour and reinforcement is crucial. The better your timing, the better the response from your dog. A reward mark allows you to reinforce behaviour at a distance.

is timing, timing, timing. Consequences must be contingent upon behaviour for the lesson to be assimilated by your dog, and fairly quickly, too. Remember that consequences must come during the behaviour or within half of a second for optimum learning.

If you apply the perfect consequences, but they are mistimed, you will not get the behaviour you were aiming for. The better your timing, the better your communication. Incorrect timing is like having serious static on the phone line—the wrong messages are being sent and received. This can also become extremely irritating and frustrating to both the student and the teacher.

You can practice training skills to improve your timing. Experiment with your clicker or other RM on your dog, horse, or cat using a behaviour that doesn't matter if it gets messed up (having your dog shake her head or step backward, etc.), rather than beginning with an obedience exercise. That will also take the pressure off of you.

To improve your timing, you can practice training skills using people as your student. People make good subjects and the "Training Game" is a fun one to play. (See the Appendix for game rules.). You elicit behaviour from your human pupil without using any spoken language at all, merely marking their behaviour with a predesignated reward mark. (If you are using a person as a victim to practice your timing on, you won't mess up your dog's head, which might be a tad more difficult to fix. The person knows you're playing a game and, hopefully, your training methods will not scar them for life.) It helps people to understand how confusing it is when no words are allowed to be used to help convey a message. People become so used to expressing themselves via the spoken word that they forget that animals don't understand spoken language (or French, Swahili, etc.). Animals tend to rely on body language to communicate with each other and with us.

We must develop alternative methods, other than words, to help the animal understand what we are expecting from him.

Timing Short Course

- Latency between behaviour and consequence must be (pick one) short, small, tiny, miniscule, infinitesimal. Use an RM/NRM (reward mark/no reward mark) system—it is the quickest way to achieve clear communication.
- For optimum results and the highest possible learning curve, the consequence must be apparent to the animal during the behaviour or within half of a second. The RM/NRM system buys you some time here. While the RM or NRM must be right on the money, they buy you time in getting the auxiliary reinforcers to your dog. That is, you can fumble in your pocket for a cookie, run to the cupboard to get the chicken bit for Spot, or get the tennis ball out of the snap thing that hangs on your belt loop.

- Watch for intention behaviour so you can be ready to apply appropriate consequences. In other words, catch the glance of attention, the pricking of the ears, and the momentary stillness that precedes the lunge at the cat.
- Pay attention and concentrate. You will not achieve good timing if you don't.
- Noncontingent timing results in random reinforce-

Be prepared to apply appropriate consequences to your dog's behaviour at all times. The timing between the behaviour and the consequence should be as short as possible.

ment and punishment. If your timing is incorrect, how will Spot possibly establish a pattern and "find Waldo?"

Failure to Generalize, or Don't Like to Travel?

This item really falls under the topic of undertraining. However, the lack of generalization of a behaviour is so common and important that I give the subject it's very own section.

How quickly the animal will generalize depends on the animal and the behaviour you are trying to get. My experience is that if the activity you are asking for is in line with Spot's instincts, tendencies, or natural abilities, the lesson will be learned almost effortlessly. So the rule is: **If the behaviour is in line with the pupil's innate tendencies, the behaviour will happen effortlessly.** To wit: Teaching your Chesapeake to swim on cue will require no effort on your part. Maybe one repetition and that behaviour will be set. (Try to keep him out of the water, and you're talking a different story.) If you are going to teach your Basset to retrieve ducks, you may have a bit more of a challenge (but I didn't say you couldn't do it...).

People depend on many extraneous cues to elicit behaviour. That is, they give

The bait bag that the trainer is wearing is a special condition, which needs to be removed in later training. This is so the dog obeys whether the food is present or not.

lots of prompts in addition to the key command or signal. Special conditions such as leaning over and clapping in addition to a verbal command "Dog, come" must be faded out. When you can stand straight up with your hands at your sides, or better yet, be out of sight entirely and still have Spot respond to just "Dog, come," you have a dog that really knows which cue—"Dog, come"—is attached to which behaviour—coming when called.

Take your dog out and about to expose him to new situations and new people. Practice his behaviour in each new location and reward him for a job well done.

Often, response to a cue is dictated by many special conditions—proximity is a big one. For example, if Spot is standing near you, he responds well to the down cue. But if he is ten feet away, he looks at you like he has never heard the word or has never set eyes on you in his life. To Spot, hearing the word at 10 feet and never hearing the word at all is pretty close to the truth. The fact that you are 10 feet away *is* different. How quickly your dog responds to this situation with the desired behaviour depends on how well he generalizes, in addition to how completely he understands the command "Down" in the first place. A common reaction is to walk closer to you and lie down. Furthermore, if a dog is always worked on leash, don't think off -leash work will happen in ten minutes. I can nearly guarantee you it won't.

Another example is when your dog performs well in one location but not in another. If you train only in one or two locations, don't expect miracles when you take Spot out and about. Given the scale of difficulty with generalization, I almost laugh when my students say to me "He should know...." And when I am saying those words to one of my training buddies, let me tell you they don't use anywhere near that restraint...I have nearly had to take Mary to the hospital. We've been in situations where she was laughing so hard I was afraid we'd need oxygen for her. I really resent it when someone repeats *my* advice back to me, as my students and friends invariably do. It's so rude, don't you think?

As a synopsis: If you want the behaviour performed in several locations, don't think you can take the behaviour in question out of your living room (or wherever you have been training Spot) and get it the first night of dog class or anywhere other than your living room. "He does this at home..." is like a mantra of first-night students. The point is that he's not doing it here and now. So get started—get the safely leashed Spot out and about. Take that puppy with you to the corner store for milk. Practice a quick sit/stay in the parking lot. In just a few extra minutes (less than five), you have started down the road to having a trained companion. But it won't happen without your effort and Spot's. It takes two to tango, remember? And teamwork is the name of the training game!

> Generalizing a behaviour is the most time-consuming issue trainers face, so face it!

Your dog may not behave in certain settings. Be aware of the events and environment around you and try to prepare for any problems before they occur.

Setting Events or Carpe Diem

Think of the behaviour as being surrounded by not only the antecedent and the consequence, but also the environment, location, and other additional conditions that inhabit the stage. **Setting events** are all of the contextual factors or any other condition that might influence behaviour. Setting events are a big problem, but they just won't go away. We and our dogs live in the real world and not in a vacuum. Since setting events are here to stay, you might as well get used to them, find out what they are, and deal with them. Setting events are the good things, too. They include the cue, the location, the context of the behaviour, and the conditions that are within the individuals who are working together. Are you hungry or cranky or happy? Is Spot hungry or satiated or already exhausted from prior activities?

What do you do about setting events? Just be aware of what they are. If you are aware of the setting events you are dealing with, you are armed and ready for action. You can control many setting events, and get control of others by preventing direct access to them. Set yourself and your dog up for success as often as possible, and give Spot feedback about the behaviour that occurs. The real world is actually a great place to be. So go out there with your dog and live! Carpe diem! Seize the day! In the context of dog training, seize the "event" and take control of it, or it will control your dog and by extension—you.

Here's a recap on things you can do:

- Be aware of setting events.
- Control the ones you can; prevent access to others.
- Think ahead—What setting events might be present? Which ones will you have to deal with? What will you do about them? For instance, for dogs that are unruly at the door, have a leash handy to manufacture and control behaviour, and have treats in a jar near the door so you can provide R+ for desired behaviour.

Contingency Issues and Establishing Operations
You Get What You Pay For

Since we have opposable thumbs and can openers and our dogs do not, they are at our mercy for all items necessary to survival, like canned dog food and ball-tossing. Since we control their environment closely to keep them safe, they are also dependent upon us for recreation.

If you give your dog every little thing he desires for free, then he probably doesn't pay much attention to you. As my daughter, when she was four years old, so succinctly put it after a visit to grandma's house: "Grandma does every little thing I want every minute of the day and night." If this sounds like you and your dog, you have not proved to him that you are relevant.

If someone would pay me lots of money to just sit at home and do as I please, I would no doubt elect to do just as I please, rather than taking care of the myriad items that I am obligated to do to bring money into the household—and I certainly wouldn't do anything resembling housework.

What I am trying to say is that you need to make Spot work for what he gets. If you make R+ contingent on behaviour, you will have a well-behaved dog. If you

Teach your dog that consequences are contingent upon behavior. Even a very young puppy like Willow can learn to sit before she is given her dinner.

hand out everything at random and/or for nothing, you may expect the same kind of behaviour back from Spot—random and/or no desirable behaviour. It happens all the time in the real world—"You get what you pay for."

Once Spot understands that the way to the food, toys, fun, games, walks, tossing the ball, etc. is through you, he very quickly comes to think of you as relevant. This is just where you want to be. Next, he should offer you behaviour that you have positively reinforced in an effort to tell you he understands your relevance in the scheme of things.

If Spot wants attention, ask for a sit first. Don't just leave a bowl of food sitting around all the time. When you feed a meal, ask for a down/stay before you put the bowl down. This makes it obvious to Spot who the fairy godmother or fairy godfather is—you! You become relevant in Spot's eyes—you have a place in the universe instead of just being part of the furniture. It becomes important for your dog to work with you—you have access to all the good stuff. Before you release Spot to play with his little dog friends, ask for a sit/stay with attention and then allow him to go play. Listen carefully—here is a big training secret disguised as common sense: **Make consequences contingent on behaviour.**

Competing Reinforcers

You might not be aware of it, but there is always a hierarchy of reinforcers present. Ask your dog—he'll tell you. You need to know what is at the top of the pyramid in this current situation for your dog, and then you need to get control of those things. When what you want and what Spot wants comes into direct conflict, you are often talking about competing reinforcers. For example, Spot is thinking: What you have doesn't look as good as that other thing that I *could* have if I just get rid of the idiot (you) who is telling me to sit.

How do you know what the competing reinforcers are? Your dog will tell you. What is currently serving as a dog magnet? The squirrel running across the park? The ice cream cone that the child walking by on the sidewalk is holding? Whatever Spot is currently looking at or straining to get to instead of paying attention to your cue is what is currently at the top of the hierarchy for Spot.

How do you get control? First, prevent any direct access strategy that Spot is using. In a very mechanical or physical way, you must make sure Spot does not get the opportunity to reinforce himself. This means you must have physical control until you have verbal control. Leashes are one way of preventing direct access. You must be in control of the R+. That means that dogs have good recall before being off leash. My puppies drag a long line for a good year or more before I let them run loose in situations where I know they can have direct access to reinforcers without getting permission first. If there is any doubt about absolute verbal control, my dogs reamain on leash. If they chased a squirrel yesterday, what makes you think that today, with no training, there will be any behaviour change? In short, you have to be in the position that you can control or "spoil" the dog's fun. While it's no fun raining on parades, it is not always appropriate to have your dog going wacko over cars, squirrels, bikes, etc. Your dog chasing down the paperboy is certainly not fun for the paperboy. Getting hit by a car is no fun for the distracted dog chasing a squirrel, rabbit, or cat. So stay in control and keep your dog safe, and establish control over his behaviour at the same time.

Always put yourself in a position where you can "spoil any fun" your dog can have without your permission. Back that up by teaching Spot that if he gives you the behaviour you want, he can have what he wants (when it is appropriate and safe); if what he wants is not appropriate or safe, you will offer another R+ as a "consolation prize." For example, your dog likes to play with other dogs. When appropriate, ask for a sit, then release him to play. Call him out of play, and as an R+ for coming to you, release him back into the play group. This all involves getting a handle on Premack behaviours. Remember: Premack's Principle is that you can R+ a low probability behaviour by allowing access to a high probability behaviour, which is a bunch of six-dollar words that mean you will allow access to behaviours Spot enjoys if he does something you want first.

Rules About Getting Your Dog's Attention

Distraction often concerns competing reinforcers, as well as just plain old looking around. Unfortunately, there is no quick fix. You have to place the dog in distracting circumstances and gradually harden the dog's attention span. The only advice I can give you that has worked for me is to use appropriate feedback

Distractions are everywhere, so you must train your dog to resist them. Breanna would love to go check out the horse, but she remains in the heel position as requested.

Breanna gets a Reward Mark while she's performing the heel. The RM gives the handler time to get the treats.

when it comes to paying attention versus not paying attention. I provide a lot of food up front in distracting circumstances. Ignoring non-attention would be my first choice. Wait for attention, then mark it and feed it. Don't walk into a new situation with your dog, stand there chatting with friends, and then be cross with him for not paying attention to you. This is not fair. When you walk into a new location, think about the song "For Your Eyes Only." (I know I am dating myself—Yes, I was a teen in the '70s.) You need to be concentrating, paying attention to your dog, and getting control over his behaviour with a sit or a down. Then you can release him to be an idiot while you socialize. Alternatives to that are standing there and giving your dog a constant feed to keep him occupied and next to you. This way you are literally conditioning your dog to pay attention to you even if you are paying attention to something else. Another option would be to put him in a down/stay. When I am with a very experienced dog, I will give him a cue word for atten-tion. If I don't get the atten-tion, I provide appropriate consequences, depending on the dog's experience level and temperament. For some dogs that means an NRM. For others that means putting my face next to theirs and giving them "what for" in the form of some eye contact and a verbal "Hello there—anybody home?" It is also effective to give a light tap on the head (Go easy. This is just a touch.) "Knock knock —anybody home?"

Lack of Inter-Command Discrimination or Make the Connection

Okay, you gave a cue (or more the way I like to think about it, made a request) and you got nothing in return. Zilch. Zero. Or you got something else that you didn't ask for in the form of another behaviour or some random behaviour that Spot just made up. What is that all about, anyway? The most recent reinforcer, total reinforcement history for a cue, what was done the last time in this context, learned patterns, competing reinforcers—all of these issues *may* take precedence over the cue you have just given the dog. Spot is guessing a lot more than you might think.

This situation is *very* common in dogs that have a repertoire of behaviours that have been reinforced, but that aren't quite sure about all the connections just yet. For instance, let's say your canine genius has just learned sit and down, but has really not yet connected the cue with the behaviour. So you request a sit and get a down. The dog has a reinforcement history with both behaviours, so he makes a wild guess. He offers something he thinks you might want in the hope of earning the R+. I always hear about the dog that knows several tricks: "So we just go near the cookie jar and Spot sits up, rolls over, then speaks—and I didn't say a word!" Maybe the last time you went to the park you played Frisbee™ with Spot, but today it's raining. For the whole walk, Spot keeps looking at you expectantly, waiting for that Frisbee™ to fly. He can't believe that all you brought was that stupid umbrella.

These are all instances of confusion. Use your no reward mark (NRM) and begin another trial with help. Just continue being consistent with your antecedent events and consequent events so that the dog learns which behaviour goes with which cue. **Patience, repetition, and feedback**. (You know, come to think of it, I could have saved myself a lot of typing and you a lot of reading if I had just given you those three words pages ago...um, never mind.)

Fear

Fear and stress can, and often do, prevent learning, and certainly interfere with optimum learning curves. This truth is too often overlooked by novice trainers

Fear and stress will be exhibited through body language and will inhibit your dog's learning processes. If your dog becomes fearful, do some easy behaviours that will build his confidence and afford him success.

and by many experienced trainers who become impatient as well. The dog must learn to bear some stress, period. But dole stress out in small amounts. Be aware of what stress looks like in your dog, and please avoid punishers in stressful situations. Likewise, avoid "buying into" or validating the fear/stress for the dog by reassuring him (he interprets your wheedling tone as R+ for his current goofy behaviour). Ignore what you don't like, R+ what you do like, and help the dog to succeed. Manage the environment and other setting events to the extent that you can, and work with what you've got.

To illustrate this, I am going to teach you all about molecular biology. (Pretend you want to know for a minute, OK?) I am going to take you to the most dangerous neighborhood I can find. You know, the kind with lots of drive-by shootings. We'll sit on the corner observing the goings on and you will learn so much...Not! You will be so worried and anxious about this whole state of affairs that you will learn nothing, except perhaps to try to avoid me and the whole situation. This is how your dog will react in a stressful situation.

Overshadowing and Blocking

When dog training (and great advice for many real-world circumstances), stay out of your own way! **Overshadowing** occurs when you·present two different signals to a dog simultaneously. One of those two signals will probably be more

Telling your dog to do one thing while your body language says something else will only serve to confuse him. Be sure to separate your cues and control your body language so overshadowing and blocking does not occur.

salient or noticeable. If you are luring the dog with a piece of food and saying, "Sit," at the same time, what do you really think the dog is paying attention to and focusing on? If you guessed the food, you get a prize! The same thing happens when you present a hand signal and a verbal signal at the same time. The dog may be cueing in on one or the other. How are you to know which one it is? You don't, until the dog makes what you think is a mistake, but he thinks is the correct behaviour. Uh oh! Confusion!

Blocking occurs when a new cue and an old cue are given simultaneously. Because there is no "new information," the dog focuses on the known cue and ignores the new cue. Then, one day you give only the new cue, and Wa La— nothing. Leash prompts and physical modeling of the animal can be big contributors to blocking, if they are given at the same time that you give another cue.

The year I trained Breanna for the American Kennel Club Companion Dog title, I used the verbal command "Swing" for Breanna to finish. I always used a happy tone of voice. One of my instructors noted in class one evening that I was using a lot of facial expression as well. The concern was that a judge might nail me for a double cue. I thanked this kind person and decided that I would carefully monitor my face. So on the next recall, I held my face very still, but said in my bright happy voice, "Bree, swing." Breanna sat there, tail going 90 mph, wearing a big smile and gazing at my face, just waiting for me to let her know what I wanted next. Puzzled, I tried again and got the same reaction. I began to have an uneasy feeling that I had somehow made a big communication error somehow, way back when. Without saying a word, I raised my eyebrows and smiled the happy face that I had used with my happy command. Breanna executed a perfect finish. The next time, I cut out the smile. I thought the cue for swing was the verbal one. For Breanna, the motion of my eyebrows was the most salient cue. Therefore, her cue and my cue were two different animals—communication glitch!

To avoid both of the above, **separate your cues** and **control your body language.** Practice your cues in front of a mirror (without the dog.) so you know that the cue you intend to attach to the behaviour is indeed understood as such by the dog. If this is happening, refer to the "Prompts and Fading" section of this book. It covers how to add new cues. If you use the recommended steps, you will not be blocking or overshadowing, and therefore giving your dog foggy cues.

conflict resolution

If you encounter a training challenge, don't get mad, don't get frustrated, don't get even. Stop, take a time out, and sit down with your notebook. Or better yet, your notebook *and* a training partner. (My own little Punch is alive today because of the timely intervention of my training partner, Mary, on numerous occasions.) Use the technical reasons discussed in earlier chapters as a checklist. Now describe why you got noncompliance. Plan your next training session accordingly. Don't be too quick to decide that you have willful disobedience. Give the dog the benefit of the doubt and exhaust all other options.

Being smart and merciful doesn't mean being permissive, however. Of course, you should not let the dog participate in activities that might harm him, you, or someone else. Above all, use your judgment to provide appropriate consequences for any behaviour. Obviously, there are some behaviours that cannot be allowed. Take care of your setting events in that case and use prevention to keep everyone safe and happy.

Resolving conflict involves forgiving. How many times has your dog forgiven you?

- What does it take to cause a conflict? There are different points of view. For example, those involved:

    1) have a different paradigm about the current situation;

    2) want a different outcome to the situation;

    3) have different ideas about what to do in the context of this situation.

- How many does it take to have a conflict?

    More than one. (At least for our purpose…)

- Conflict is part of life. Accept it. Figure out how to best cope with it.
- When faced with conflict the two parties may try the following strategies:

  1) Avoidance.

  2) Aggression.

  3) Working together to resolve the conflict.
- How to solve conflict:

  1) Calm down—take time to cool off if required.

  2) Identify the source of the conflict and the exact problem.

  3) Devise a strategy. Solutions are the name of the game. Problem solve. Use lateral thinking, not linear thinking.

  4) Weigh the solutions: What will happen if I do this? Will both parties get what they need with this solution? Who or what else might be affected by the solution?

  5) Choose the solution. Carry it out. Did it work or not? Why?

Communication is the Key

Be a good listener. What is your dog trying to tell you? Remember that dogs rely on some very subtle body language to talk to each other. That is also how your dog will attempt to communicate with you. The slight motion of moving their eyes to the side, the slight turn of the head, the small shift from one hip to the other—by using these gestures, they may be trying to open the lines of communication with you. You won't be able to rely on your ears for this task. You must become Sherlock Holmes—Observe and learn!

> To effectively communicate with your dog:
> - Don't adopt a defensive body posture—you're calm, remember?
> - Smile. (At the very least: Don't scowl).
> - Keep your arms relaxed (not on your hips or folded in a defensive posture).

Once the dog makes a mistake, I have seen many a student destroy the dog's attitude by maintaining a chronic low level of punishment directed toward the dog. How did they convey this to their dog? By allowing their own emotional baggage, consisting of frustration and disappointment, to be taken out on the dog. The dog doesn't know that you are probably frustrated with yourself—he just knows that you are frustrated. Past experiences have taught him that he usually gets the blame when you are frustrated. It doesn't matter what the real reason is, he expects to be the fall guy. Even if you haven't punished him, many dogs are so very sensitive to us that they feel distressed by our attitudes. That is one advantage to my Smooths. They figure that my mental health is my own problem, and they don't concern themselves with it, even on those occasions that it might be appropriate to do so. My German Shepherd Dog is somewhat different than that, worrying about my slightest mood change.

Here are some pointers on giving correction effectively:

1) Give appropriate feedback to the dog without being brutal or abusive.

2) Use appropriate consequences. If a punisher is in order, so be it—but please tailor the measures to the crime and to the dog, not to your own emotions.

3) Be clear with your communications.

4) Use good timing.

5) Make consequences contingent on behaviour.

6) Remain neutral if the dog gets it wrong. Save being emotional for when the dog gets it right.

7) If you need to take a break because if the dog gives you one more incorrect response you may do something very drastic, put the dog in a crate, sit down, and have a lemonade. Try again tomorrow or in 10 minutes, whenever you have regained your perspective.

Teamwork for a Winning Solution

The key to effective training is negotiation—it's you and me, buddy. You and the dog work it out together. If negotiation isn't working, try mediation—get a dog trainer or behavioural consultant to help you figure out the problem. The person you get to help you should be looking for upbeat, humane solutions to your training problem that are fair to both you and your dog.

a reprise—something old, something new

The Three Phases of Learning

First, educate yourself. The objective of training your dog is to develop the skills necessary to communicate with him in a way that promotes understanding on both sides. You are not a dog and he is not a human, so there's a bit of learning that must take place on both your parts. You must learn to speak "dog" to the best of your ability, and the dog must learn to respond to your communications. Nobody starts out bilingual—it is an acquired skill.

The best way to develop these communication skills (in both of you) is to help the dog learn by association with the use of primary and secondary stimuli. Keep your training sessions short, fun, and interesting. Trainer boredom leads to dog boredom. Give up those inhibitions—live a little! Look and act interesting. Smile. Communicate with that dog. See, you can do it!

With pet dogs, I emphasize life rewards (the Premack Principle) as well as food. While it is the same with my competition dogs, I never get rid of the primary reinforcer—food. I am asking for precise and specific behaviours, darned few of which make sense to the dog. This is really my game, and I just want the dog to play, too. Because my dogs enjoy their obedience work, many of the cues and exercises themselves become reinforcing. For dogs that love to retrieve, picking up the dumbbell is reinforcing. If you have made coming to you a consistently pleasant experience, that can also be reinforcing. As you randomize the reinforcement schedule and provide reinforcement variety, you will begin to see your dog becoming reliable and responsible.

The Three Phases of Training Behaviour

In order to teach your dog, you need to know a bit about how a dog learns. Training is split up into three separate and fairly distinct phases:

Teaching / Learning

Improving / Generalizing

Polishing/ Challenging

Teaching / Learning

The first phase of training is teaching/learning. You, the trainer, might be learning new skills, too. Be patient with yourself, as well as with Spot. Sure, you'll both make mistakes, but that's okay. You're a team; you can forgive each other. Using this attitude can help both of you to avoid frustration. You'll probably still encounter some teeth-grinding at some point. I always do! But keep in mind that this is just dog training—not life and death. For me, it's what I do for fun.

Avoid stress and anxiety in learning by using the following formula.

1) Elicit the Behaviour

I often use a lure during this stage. The objective is to get the dog to understand the "position" or "concept" of the target behaviour. Sometimes opportunity training is the best way, or an action on your part that produces a reaction on the dog's part. Modeling (physically manipulating the dog into a position) is an option also, although my personal experience has shown that many animals find this so distracting that it has limited uses. The only rule here is to get the behaviour. (It should be implied but not spoken that the behavior is obtained by inducive means rather than coercive means. Obtain a voluntary reaction from Spot.)

2) Put the Behaviour on Cue

When you can get the behaviour, put it on cue. Have your cue figured out and practiced ahead of time without the dog, so Spot can count on a consistent command and/or signal. (Just a quick reminder: I am using the terms command and signal as the AKC Obedience Rule Book does. Command is specifically a verbal cue. Signal is a specific hand signal with no verbal "help." When preparing for competition, sometimes you are allowed to use both; other times only one or the other.)

3) Got It!

At this stage you have a **baby behaviour**. At this point the dog understands the position/concept of the exercise and is performing the behaviour on cue reliably, albeit with some help.

Improving/Generalizing

1) Raise the Criteria

Step by step, increase the complexity of the exercise. You will begin to "fade" your cue so that you end up with what you want your final cue to be. You continue shaping the behaviour toward your end goal.

2) Generalize

Take that behaviour "on the road." Taking a baby behaviour on the road when you are still accustomed to providing a lot of help and support to Spot is a helpful thing to do. It helps to generalize the behaviour with less effort and time invested. I think it also helps prevent trainer frustration because you're not going "back to kindergarten from grad school" quite so often, as when you train the behaviour to perfection in one area, then have to move it to another area and start over. (By the way, if you only practice in one area, location, or context, don't expect Spot to be able to make a quantum leap with that behaviour when you go to another location or change the context in some other way.)

Generalizing the behaviour will teach Spot to concentrate and will build self-confidence in both you and your dog. You come to understand what Spot is capable of and when, and he can determine the same about you; you can depend on each other's behaviour. You will see Spot truly begin to understand the exercise in any context. Practice prepares Spot to respond to you, even in

Once your dog is performing correct behaviours on a consistent basis, slowly increase the complexity of the exercises and continue shaping his behaviour toward your end goal.

stressful or excitable situations where he would normally feel so overwhelmed and distracted that he may not be able to respond. You will be excited when you see the light go on. Actually, excited is sort of an understatement; ecstatic, agog, and proud begin to come closer to the emotion. All of the effort necessary to get the correct behaviour will be worth it when you see your dog responding consistently to your cues in a variety of situations.

Part of practice is introducing distractions. A distraction, or as I prefer, a **challenge**, is anything that changes the context of the exercise for the dog. This can seem simple to you—maybe you do no more than change the location where the exercise has been consistently performed. For some dogs, the really good discriminators, tying your shoes differently seems to make a difference in their perception of the exercise. For Spot, each distraction is an entirely new problem. Each new challenge will require some time before the dog becomes reliable in that situation. Dogs, in general, are very sensitive to context. By helping the dog succeed with distraction work, we teach him to generalize his behaviour. This helps Spot to develop enough self-confidence to be reliable in many situations.

Dog trainers call this process **proofing**. Proofing makes that whole idea of picking out the pattern of when to do what behaviour clearer to your dog. Like fishermen want to set the hook, proofing sets the cue in the dog's mind.

This work also brings into the open all of the dog's ideas about how the exercise should be done. (This is a good thing. It's better to find out what Spot is thinking in a training session, rather than out in the obedience ring or when you are demonstrating tricks for your friends.) When the dog gives an incorrect response, he is most often asking you a question: "Is *this* how we do it?" Your response should be to guide him in the right direction. Remember, save corrections for situations when willful disobedience is the issue. You wouldn't (or at least I hope you wouldn't) slap a child who asks you a question; but the questions our dogs ask us in the only way they know how are met with punishment on a regular basis. If Spot is asking you a question, which is very common in early stages of learning a behaviour, please help him out. Don't be cross! Give Spot the benefit of the doubt—don't you like it when others cut you some slack? (p.s.—I bet your dog has cut you slack on many an occasion when you didn't deserve it.)

It is so fascinating to watch a dog's interpretations of what we want. One of my finest times was with Breanna at a match, rather than a trial. (Thank heaven! A match is like practice for the real thing—the real thing being an obedience trial at a dog show.) It was our first time in open obedience. We walked into the ring and readied ourselves to begin. The judge said, "Forward." I said, "Heel," and

Breanna took off like a shot, veered across the ring, flew over the high jump, tore over to the far corner of the ring, twirled around in mid-air, and did a perfect drop. Her whole manner intimated: "This is always how I respond to 'Heel' ." The look on the judge's face was worthy of a Kodak moment. Even I was a bit stunned by this maneuver—it was right at the top limit, even for Breanna. She lie there in her perfect sphinx down, a big smile on her face, her metronome tail going at 90 miles an hour. She was so proud of herself for being ever so clever. It was all I could do to keep a straight face, and the rest of the crowd wasn't even trying. I didn't dare laugh too hard, lest I reinforce her behaviour and then I'd be stuck with it for good. So I called her back, and then we did the pattern the AKC way, which I must admit was quite a bit more boring than Breanna's interpretation. Lots of people said, "What a good sport" etc., but you know I wasn't being a good sport at all. That dog was so pleased with herself that there was no possible way I could have felt good about raining on her parade. It is certainly disappointing when you've spent your entry fee, training time, travel time, and on and on, to have your dog make such a fool of you! But your dog doesn't see it that way at all. Breanna was blissfully unaware of the time, money, and effort I spent to get her into the obedience ring. All she knew was that she was out having a good time with Mom.

During challenge work, you may see some of the following responses from your dog.

Lack of Confidence

Dog: "I can't do this because I'm afraid I won't succeed."

The dog begins, but backs off.

Avoidance

Dog: "I can't cope with this."

The dog leaves the scene entirely.

Freezing

Dog: "If I don't do anything, maybe it will all go away."

This is a "flight" (fear) response—go easy! Help your dog, don't correct him.

Distraction

Dog: "Wow! You/it/they look like fun!"

The dog ignores you and the exercise and goes to the distraction. This is generally a happy-go-lucky, confident response. By teaching focus and concentration, this type of response can be overcome.

Anticipation

Dog: "I understand the exercise, and I'm eager to show you how clever I am!"

Do not correct your dog! Spot is beginning to understand. You must be the good teacher.

The next time you give the command, be ready to intervene at that moment of anticipation. That might mean having your dog on leash or a variety of other techniques, varying with the situation.

Success

Yes! Stop—you got what you asked for, and there will be many more times you can give the command, but not today. This is a good place to leave the dog's mind—on that *new, great, correct* effort. So, celebrate!

Any time you change the complexity of the exercise, it becomes an entirely new exercise from Spot's point of view. You have, in his eyes, just changed the rules. He won't hold this against you. If you have laid the proper base for your training, he will see it as a new and fun game and rise to the challenge. By alternately challenging and guiding, you encourage Spot's problem-solving ability, which strengthens Spot's self-confidence and helps him to make the right decisions. Be patient and wait for Spot's responses. He can usually figure it out, and that is very exciting to see!

Remember that challenge work is used to build self-confidence in both trainer and dog. You come to depend on each other's reactions. However, be careful with challenge work. If, for instance, you have a sound-sensitive dog, tape a dog show and slowly play it back at increasing volume. Pair the whole process with lots of R+. Challenges are not a chance to trick your dog. The purpose of using challenges in training is to **harden the response,** so that Spot is prepared to obey you in all situations. Common sense is the rule. If Spot is becoming stressed, back off. The purpose here is to present problems to

Reinforcement training will build self-confidence and promote a feeling of teamwork.

Spot so he can learn that crucial discrimination/generalization balance that tells him what to do when.

Polishing/Challenging

This polishing phase is for those going on to compete. In this phase, the handler must eliminate any extra signals or body language that he is giving Spot, and both dog and trainer must conform to the exact requirements of competition obedience, agility, herding, schutzhund, etc. Remember **fading and special conditions?** Spot must learn to perform as he would in the show ring, where he won't be allowed any help from the handler. The handler must hone his skills so no points are deducted for handler error. Know your rules! Have a grasp of how the judging is performed and what the judges look for. Go to as many matches and show and go's as you possibly can.

I know, you can't take food into the ring or give correction in any form, and in the higher classes, you leave your leash with the steward as well. But there are lots of things that you can take into the ring with you—your consistent cues, your smile, and the relationship that you have so carefully nurtured with your dog. You also have all of the body language that Spot depends on for security, and the reinforcement history that you have built up. Will you succeed? Yes. Will you ever get a nonqualifying score? Probably, at some time or another. Will it be the end of the world? No. I learn from every mistake I make, and my dog's responses in the ring are entirely dependent on the training (or lack thereof) that I have done and the cues I have given—in addition to the clay I was given in the form a dog. Clay with some of it's own ideas...I know, I know. It is easy to take Spot's responses personally. That is a common trap to fall into. If you get an incorrect response, go back to the drawing board. Once over the initial disappointment, I can always trace my error to some training mistake or handler error I have committed. Remember, you're the one in charge here, not Spot. While my dogs enjoy competition and training because I have made it fun, they would be just as content to be lying on my lap or running in the woods. What they really like is being with me!

By relying on motivation instead of correction and/or coercion to teach, your dog enjoys the training and you experience the joy of teamwork and the development of a deeper bond with your friend. A long-term commitment based on understanding—isn't that why you got a dog in the first place?

it's always, "sit, stay, heel," never, "be imaginative, be inventive, be yourself"

For those of us who have dogs that think Lassie is a dork, this note is for you. Having done my share of rescue work, having owned a commercial kennel and having done in-home consultations, on top of living with a pack of Smooth Fox Terrorists and with girls who have decided they detest each other and boys who are determined to allow testosterone to direct their behaviour, I can tell you that the very best way to deal with independent (read hard-headed, don't listen, stubborn, impossible, have a mind of their own, run off, don't know I'm alive) dogs is with a very high reliance upon R+. These dogs have their own agenda and are already uninterested in rescheduling their activities to accommodate yours. Their dance card is already full. The best way to deal with active (read hyper, bouncing off the wall, perpetual motion, the attention span of a gnat) dogs is with a very high reliance upon R+. Active dogs can also be very sensitive, and sometimes the high activity level itself is due to a lot of anxiety issues your dog may have. Punishers increase the anxiety, which increases the activity level, which usually gets Spot punished. The best way to deal with dogs that have a low activity level (read dead, uninterested, should be hired out for use as inert objects) is—guess! Yes! R+. If anything is going to get that dog off the sofa, it's going to have to be something worth getting off the sofa for. My question always is: If R+ works so well for difficult animals (read impossible to use force with or get anywhere with), why not use it with the animals that are relatively easy to train?

All dogs are social predator/scavenger types. Get some books on wolf behaviour. Although very different from wolves, our domestic dogs have some similarities with them; they use body language that wolves use. There is also some excellent stuff out there on dog behaviour. Ethology, for instance, is the study of just observing behaviour and writing it down. The behaviourists, of course, are the crowd that is not content to just watch the behaviour—they feel obligated to change behaviour. Both groups have a lot to offer you on the road to understanding your dog for the wonderful perfect creature he or she is.

Please remember that we have selectively bred many breeds to be independent, to think for themselves, and to be good problem solvers. However, sometimes we are complaining about the very thing we have carefully selected for. Do some research before you take on the responsibility of

All dogs were originally scavengers, an inherent trait that is proudly upheld by dogs to this day.

training and living with a different species. By research, I mean search out those who are knowledgeable about the breed you are interested in and talk to them. Speak with as many of the following as possible about your breed: pet people, show people, breeders, veterinarians, professional groomers, or kennel owners. Professionals know how these dogs behave under stress and are not as biased toward any one breed as a breeder might be. Rescue groups give out good information as well. Much more important than many people realize is the issue of recovery or rebound. How quickly does the individual dog recover from stress and how well does he cope with ongoing stress? Choose resources carefully. In the Appendix, I have listed books that I have found useful for dog selection. For example, although I had read that terriers were lively, that didn't cover the half of it. And when I read that they were loyal, I took it to mean that the dog would acknowledge my presence without my having to throw a party for him first. That's why talking to those who are familiar with the breed is a necessary addition to book worming. I have helped many people avoid a terrible, tragic error by allowing them to come over and interact with my Smooths. If they can meet Punch and are still interested, I know they will be okay coping with the breed. And then there are those folks who might be better suited to a cat or a goldfish!

In the case where all of this research is too late (like it was for me), because you already went to look at puppies, check out the original track record and breeding history of your breed of choice. This process will give you a lot of insight into why your dog behaves the way he does.

It is important to know what traits your breed was selected for. Some of the behaviours you may find frustrating are inherited behaviors.. Many behaviours that are interpreted as being a "problem" are very natural for our dogs. If you are aware of a dog's natural propensities, you can be prepared to deal with them— either tolerating, managing, training, or more likely, a combination of the three. For example, hounds were bred to follow their noses and take off, and it's our job to keep up with them. Vocalizations (howling and barking) allow the two-leggers to keep track of the four-leggers, so take a wild guess about who is out in front there. And thank god rabbits run in circles, otherwise many of us might never see

Some breeds may have inherited characteristics that you may find do not fit into your lifestyle. For instance, these Foxhounds have the natural tendency to bay and chase game, traits that may not be ideal for someone with limited space or close neighbors.

our Beagles again. You should know what the specific breed traits are in order to choose the dog that is right for you and in order to train your dog effectively.

For example, some breeds are not meant for everyone, like "go to ground" terriers and Dachshunds, both bred to kill vermin, much of which is underground. Think about the kind of personality that enjoys claustrophobic spaces underground and not only engages in hand-to-hand combat to the death at the drop of a hat, but really, really likes it. A friend of mine expressed the spirit of the Terrier Group very succinctly once: "They are like 007—terriers have a license to kill." The larger terriers were also bred to take down various game, so they have a strong dose of predation and aggression in their character. Not everyone wants to deal with this type of personality. Always shocking to me, however, is how wonderful terriers are with people. If you've ever seen terriers on game, you can fully appreciate how sweet they are with humans and how stable their temperaments really are.

Many of the non-sporting breeds that were bred to do a wide variety of jobs are

This Kuvasz patiently guards his flock. This same guarding behaviour may not be welcomed if you are unprepared to channel and manage it.

Although toy dogs are small in stature, they can be very big in attitude. No matter what the size of your breed, training is imperative to produce a canine good citizen.

a bit difficult, as well. English Bulldogs definitely fall into the low activity category, but with a healthy amount of independence thrown in. Start pushing around a 70-pound short guy who doesn't give a rip about your importance to begin with and see how far you get. There are many more in this group that might not be a piece of cake to train.

In the Herding Group, you have some very trainable sorts, and then you have the flock guardians that are quite independent and territorial. No light-duty animals these—back in the old days they watched the sheep by themselves and didn't depend on help. After all, the poor shepherd had to sleep sometime.

In the Working Group, you have that interesting crowd of nordic dogs. They were bred to run and pull, both of which they do admirably. They are big, independent, and can be territorial, as well.

The Toy Group, while small, seems for the most part to be a crowd of little Napoleons. Being bred to be good companions and lap dogs is just the excuse given. Actually, no one could begin to attempt to handle these animals if they were 60 pounds instead of the lightweights that they are! I'm just joking here, but you will find some tyrants in this group. Yorkies among them—small, but all terrorist. Pomeranians are an independent little bunch, too. And harsh physical corrections are absolutely out of bounds for these animals—it is too easy to injure them because of their small size. I will never forget a client dropping off a small, less than 10-pound Papillon mix to board for the first time. "She is very sensitive," he stated. "She is so small, and I got her from the Humane Society, so she gets worried very easily." As he said his goodbyes, the small black and white bundle of fluff licked his face and made ingratiating noises. However, as the owner's car pulled reluctantly down the drive, Miranda immediately changed her persona and began giving "Heil, Miranda" lessons. What a character! Talk about a pushy, confident little dog that knew just how to manipulate each and every individual she encountered—human and canine—to suit her little fancy. This was a very bright little pooch and a dictator in her own right.

In general, the Sporting, Herding, and Working Groups are a very cooperative crowd. They were bred to work with

Although different breeds do exhibit similar behaviours, each dog is an individual and should be treated as such.

humans bringing game to hand, moving sheep, protecting their territory, or pulling loads. But even among the so-called "natural obedience dogs" we find those individuals that march to their own drummer. If you have one of these characters, it is doubly embarrassing because everyone has told you "how trainable" the breed is. It's one thing to have a Basset or a Scottish Terrier that is hard-headed. Dog trainers pretty much expect it and are pleasantly surprised on those occasions they find it not to be so. (When presented with these individuals, I, personally, begin to tremble in excitement and anticipation.) But when your Golden, Sheltie, or Lab, falls into the difficult- dog category, eyebrows are raised askance. And I have clients who feel guilty because of it: "But this breed was supposed to be so easy to train...."

My experience is that it is never entirely the dog's fault—it takes two to tango. Sometimes the techniques being used for that particular dog are just not suitable. Across the board, I have had the absolute best results using R+. Remember that understanding learning theory gives you information about when and how to best apply appropriate consequences. Lean heavily toward the R+ end of the scale to get the ideal results. The more you use R+, the better the results you obtain will be. Personally, I find that the better the trainer I become, the more I rely on R+. I very seldom need to use any sort of aversives at all. My own training challenge is figuring out how much I can get done with R+, while paring the aversives down to nil. This method can work for you, too.

take the challenge

The step to crossing over to positive reinforcement training is a difficult one for many people to take. They have relied on other techniques for so long. Go ahead! Jump in! It's not nearly as shocking as you thought it would be. I had to literally put away the leash. I was trying hard to figure out this R+ stuff, but when I left the leash on my dog, I was correcting out of habit. So I put a drag line on to keep the dogs safe or worked in fenced areas. (A drag line is a light line 20-40 feet long that you hook to the collar so you can keep your dog safe when in an unfenced area. I go to the hardware store and get polypropylene rope; it takes the weather well and is very lightweight or, when appropriate, you can just allow your leash to drag.) It is very liberating to take that leash off and get those desired behaviours. The leash is just one less item to juggle while I'm training.

The first thing I discovered was that placement of reinforcement is a crucial point. Wherever you have fed that dog, there he will return. If you are luring Spot into heel position, have your hand where you want Spot's head to be. Likewise with everything else: What you put cookies on, you will see repeated. It's one of the rules.

Mostly, you have to be brave and begin to use the techniques I have set down. No matter how you train, the rules of behaviour are *the rules*. Operant conditioning is all about clear communication and appropriate consequences. The communication and the consequences are not some decision that *you* make based on anthropomorphism and emotion. The real story is all about educating yourself to what it takes to communicate effectively with another species. The practical application comes with doing. And the trip is so much more fun!

I had gone from training horses to training dogs and had the misfortune of hooking up with a very compulsive trainer. I am thankful that I didn't correct nearly as much or as hard as I was encouraged to do so. I more or less bullied Breanna through her Companion Dog training. (Ineptly I might add, though she got through with quite a bit of style, considering.) We began open obedience work, and she quit cold. The day that I picked up my leash to train her and she ran in the opposite direction, it dawned on me that this coercion not only made me feel uncomfortable, but it was ruining the relationship that I had with my dog. In order to avoid the confusion and punishment, she also opted to avoid me. And instead of thinking for myself, I was blindly following someone's advice, which didn't feel right. I decided that if this was how I had to do the work, I wasn't going to compete. Also, I didn't train horses this way, so what exactly was I doing? The result of the soul-searching that Breanna prompted me to do got me thinking that they couldn't possibly correct killer whales or sea lions this way. And if exotic and marine mammal trainers can get the job done with animals that are not even domesticated, then surely I can train my domestic dog by applying the same kinds of techniques. I found the book, *Don't Shoot the Dog,* by Karen Pryor, quite by accident in the library while looking for something to help me out. Bingo! A light bulb lit up! It was earth shaking! This was what I had been looking for. I began stumbling around trying to apply the principles outlined in the book and was doing so pretty clumsily, but still getting awesome results. I had changed instructors and began working with a very experienced trainer, Lillian Culp, who had been in dogs forever. She pointed me and many others in the right direction. I told her about my discovery and my curiosity about how to apply this operant conditioning stuff correctly, and she said "Well, if you want to train with food, go see Patty Ruzzo." Lillian, as an instructor, always allowed me lots of room to experiment, while still offering guidance. I did and, finally, much of the practical application of this technique became a great deal clearer to me. That was in 1994. Patty and everyone else who trains with food have become much more sophisticated in the application since then, including me and my training partner and co-experimenter, Mary.

I finally went cold-turkey and tossed away all my slip and pinch collars. I got much better results right away. Then I started using food more. Randomly and clumsily at first, then with more and more precision and expertise. Like all other skills, you have to:

1) Believe you can, and

2) Do it!

In the Appendix, I have listed the books and videos that I have found to be most helpful. However, I recommend going to seminars where you can see and experience the 3-D versions of these books and videos. Choose these carefully. Overall, you will probably find some tricks to add to your bag, even if you may not totally agree with the philosophy of the person giving that particular seminar. Over time you will develop your own philosophy.

I hesitate to even relate the following story. (Like when you're in a social gathering—if you remain quiet and keep nodding wisely, no one will suspect that you don't have a clue what they are talking about. But, since I never follow my own advice, I tend to put my silly self right out there on display. So enjoy my embarrassing moment and please learn from it.)

When I got my dog, Dervish, as a puppy, I got so carried away by the heady feeling of the "no leash" theory, that I was determined and excited to do all of his training off leash. Although it was a great idea, dogs *do* have to wear leashes and collars to get by in our society—a thought that should have and occasionally did actually enter my head. Being a professional procrastinator and endless optimist, I just never did anything about it. We were having so much fun doing other stuff. We live out in the country, which is a great excuse to be lazy because everything is fenced for the dogs, and I am not forced to walk my dogs on a leash. So, Dervish is doing great with his little collar and drag line. I am really proud, because *I* am getting so good with R+ that I never even have to pick up that line. I have our relationship and reinforcement history in order. I am becoming smug because I feel so clever that this puppy is so perfect. Enter stage left: Our first puppy match and disaster, both chortling joyfully hand-in-hand. I will not go through the gruesome event in too much detail, but do want to make a point of my naiveté. I thought because Dervish would stay right by me in any situation (even puppy class situations), I wouldn't really have to use a show lead much. I had a few brief moments of sheer panic on my drive to the match thinking "I probably should have put that martingale lead on him before today..." Well, inevitably, he got excited about being around so many strange dogs. His testosterone and natural exuberance took hold of his tiny brain and, in spite of my best efforts, Dervish hit the end of that lead and gave himself a good correction. My spoiled little mama's boy immediately threw a temper tantrum, just as I had inadvertently taught him to do. The sad fact is that I really did know better (hand to forehead). I went home most rickety-tic and taught Dervish carefully and positively about the leash thing.

This story reiterates that what you need your dog to know, you **must** teach him! Don't take it for granted that because you love Spot and you've done half of the homework, that the rest will just fall into place. It won't. Patient and consistent training will help create a well-behaved and loyal companion and will strengthen the bond between dog and owner. Humans, please generalize this behaviour!

don your humor hat and zip up your patience suit

The following items are for *your* attitude. Thinking in these ways may help you to approach training sessions with patience, perseverance, and a fun attitude.

Define expectations in single short-term goals and build these into long-term goals. This will guarantee successful feelings about yourself and your abilities, as well as the joy of having your partner succeed.

Offer short-term or frequent reinforcement, even when on the variable reinforcement schedule. **Good trainers are generous!** (If you don't understand "generous," look it up in *Webster's*. Now practice it with your dog.) You don't always need to dole out endless food once the behaviour is on a maintenance schedule, but do provide lots of positive feedback. Even in the learning laboratory, where you can engineer the environment to minimize distraction, a variable schedule for maze running rats is often 75 percent primary reinforcement to maintain the optimum performance (speed and accuracy). Remember how this particular item caused me, personally, a lot of frustration? (Even if you don't, I sure do!) It wasn't until I started tailoring the variable and intermittent schedule to the individual animal that I began to have more success. Each dog is different, but my Fox Terrorists do not do well with certain behaviours on a long or thin schedule. For example, when it comes to retrieving, my dog Breanna, despite years of R+ on this behaviour, will do three or four retrieves and if no primary reinforcement is forthcoming, I begin to see little, subtle portions of the exercise begin to crumble. One thing I definitely learned is not to drill behaviours—if my dogs get it right, we move right on to something else. Dogs differ, but I don't see my Fox Terriers maintaining formal obedience behaviours on the same kind of variable reinforcement schedule that I would use for your average Sheltie, Golden, or German Shepherd Dog.

Comparatively, my Shepherd works for very little primary reinforcement, very quickly moving on to a variable schedule. She just likes to have me tell her what to do all the time. Getting a command is in and of itself reinforcing for her. Not so with my Fox Terrorists—their attitude often seems to be "Have your people get with my people…maybe we can do lunch sometime and negotiate the details for that down/stay." That's a humorous way to look at it, but there is no doubt that I spend a lot more time hardening and lengthening the attention span of my terriers and obtaining consistent results than I do with most of the other breeds I have worked with.

In addition to the Terrier Group, other animals that fall into this category are some of the Non-Sporting Group and I would say all of the Hound Group. Some

As a trainer, you should approach all new learning experiences with a positive attitude, lots of patience, and a good sense of humor.

Off-leash training should be practiced in safe fenced-in areas and on a long line as early as possible in your dog's training.

of the flock or guardian types can be pretty strong-minded dogs, as well the large working/guarding crowd that need extra socialization long past adolescence, though they are pretty cooperative as a whole. Teaching any guarding dog judgment in any human environment has its definite pitfalls. As far as your dog is concerned, the reasons his breed was originally selectively bred for are still valid. They don't know that their job may have become obsolete. Genetics *and* environment will play a role in the clay you are given to work with—namely, the natural animal that is your dog.

up, down, or sideways?

Vertical or linear methods of problem solving are different from horizontal or random methods of problem solving. But you already know that. (Especially those of us truly random-types who have acquired a linear-type to cohabitate with!) Linear thinkers tend to follow Step 1, Step 2, Step 3, Step 4, etc., whereas a random thinker might go from Step 1 to Step 4. For example, if a vertical problem solver comes to a locked door, he might try pushing against the door, pushing harder on the door, knocking on the door, maybe even kicking in the door to gain entry. A horizontal problem solver will immediately try other methods of entry—windows, digging under the door, climbing up on the roof to see if he can get in that way. Both methods of problem solving are useful, depending on the situation. Think of it in dog training terms—if you want to get an TD and TDX title, you want a dog that tracks footsteps, which would be a vertical problem-solving method so the dog finds all "clues." However, if you want your dog to do search and rescue, you want him to reach victims by whatever means he can, as quickly as possible. In this case, a dog that air scents and ground scents is valuable—an example of horizontal problem solving. What methods do you use to problem solve most often? How about your dog—how does Spot problem solve?

You will meet dogs that excel in one or the other type of thinking, just as you would humans. It is interesting to note that quite often the breeds that rate highest on problem solving will rate lowest in obedience. Being a random thinker myself, I have the most trouble being consistent with antecedents and with following step-by-step procedures, something my dog, Punch, really needs. On the other hand, I can be very impulsive (read unpredictable), which is good for a variable reinforcement schedule.

it's the journey that counts

The message I would most like to impart to you with this brief final note is that the journey can be a good time! We humans tend to focus so much on the end goal—for example, lining those shelves with obedience trophies. I am not saying that the goal is not important. In fact, it is the first step in training. The goal can keep you motivated to carry on, but be kind to yourself and your friend getting there. I know that there have been many times in training that I have felt frustrated and less than satisfied with my training partner, and in extension, myself. If I'm the trainer and I'm not getting the behaviour, I need to look at myself first. Let's face it, Punch could care less if she presents the dumbbell from a sit or just spits it out at my feet. The latter is much easier to do! I will never forget the look on my Breanna's face during training when we got to the point of retrieving a thrown dumbbell. Her look of disgust eloquently told me, "If you wanted it, why the heck did you throw it out there in the first place?!" Her thoughts were so obvious to me that I had to laugh. She certainly had a point!

Using applied operant conditioning, I have learned so much about myself and how I, as well as my pets, learn and maintain behaviour. One of the items I most like about using techniques that rely on R+ and being aware of the laws of learning is that the journey became a fascinating arena in which to enrich the relationship that I have with my dogs. But don't just restrict yourself to using this with your dog, try it on your other pets and family. And don't forget yourself. It's a great reason to indulge in a reward like chocolate—just make sure it's contingent on behaviour!

For me, learning about learning is a process that continues. And while I'd like to have titles to my credit, that aspect of dog training has become less important to me than the learning journey itself. I am finding that I get just as big a kick out of teaching my dogs to "give me five" or "dance" as I do competing in the obedience ring, even though that was my original intention. I wanted to find a way to train my dog for competitive obedience that made me feel good and was fun for both of us. For myself and my pets, this was the way that opened door after door, and we continue to grow and have fun as we learn. I hope that by sharing my journey with others, I can help them benefit from my mistakes—and lordy I have made plenty of those! I am just grateful that I have forgiving dogs! And that is one of the other advantages I have found to training with lots of R+. If I make a mistake, Punch gets no cookie or a free cookie. Big deal—she still learns. I may have slowed the learning curve somewhat with my clumsiness, but that's about the extent of the damage I will do. The big "R"—our relationship—remains unscathed.

Woofs and wags and, most of all, happy training! Give that dog love and a cookie from me!

appendix

the training game

The training game is a great eye-opener. I was introduced to it via books and videos by Karen Pryor and have used it very successfully in my classes. The human componenent of the team really gets a feel for what its like to be the trainee instead of the trainer. It is a great way to improve timing and decision making during training without confusing and frustrating your dog.

Training contingencies are where it's at. At least two people are required, but it is lots of fun to have six or eight people in a group. In each group, one person is selected to be the "animal" and one person is selected to be the "trainer." The animal goes out of hearing range. The rest of the group chooses a behaviour for the trainer to shape. Every person in the group ideally gets to experience each position.

It is best if you choose very easy behaviours to shape initially. You may get more ambitious later if you get really good at it. You will be practicing many new skills, so shaping easy behaviours in the beginning is less frustrating for both trainer and animal. The behaviours should be physically easy for the animal and easy for everyone to observe. Some suggestions: turn in a circle, pick up an object, have the animal touch his nose or the top of his head, jump up and down, stand on one foot, raise an arm in the air, wave bye-bye, etc. Again, at first, avoid two- or three-step behaviours. You can work on behaviour sequences later when you've had some practice.

Be polite and socially acceptable. Do not invade another person's personal space, etc.

The trainer uses a predesignated reward mark, like a specific word or a clicker.

Each time the animal hears the sound, he must walk over to the trainer and get the real or imagined treat. This way you don't have an animal that just stands there trying to figure out what he just did right, thereby giving you nothing to apply R+ to.

There should be no talking! The point is that shaping is a nonverbal process. Acceptable, however, are groans, laughter (especially laughter, it burns a lot of calories and makes you younger), applause, and other encouraging, but nonword-type noises. Again, be polite and tasteful.

Once the behaviour is effectively shaped, the animal becomes the trainer and the next animal goes out of earshot and the process begins again.

You will probably see your animal get very frustrated. Work through it if you can; if not, stop and discuss why the animal is getting so frustrated. Then start again and see if you can work through the problem.

If you are stuck fast, you might try some of the following suggestions to get unstuck:

- Try a new, easier behaviour. Once the animal is working with confidence again, having had some success under his belt, go back to trying to shape the original behaviour.

- Try using a prop or prompt (nonverbal) of some sort. If you need someone to touch the top of their head, you might mess up their hair a bit. When they reach up to straighten it out, reinforce that. To get someone to go to a certain location you might place a chair or other object there that they might be curious enough about to go investigate. Once you have "lured" them into the area, you can R+.

- Make sure you aren't trying to shape a chain, and, therefore, training two behaviours simultaneously. This will only give you trouble until you break the sequence into it's smaller steps.

- Change the location—take the group into another room or another area. Often this will get the animal "working" again, especially if they were obsessing about returning to a particular object or location in the environment.

- Once you have done some of this, you can try variations. Results can be very interesting.

- Add a cue. The behaviour and cue are chosen. It is the trainer's job to select from offered behaviour or manufactured behaviour, place it under stimulus control by adding a cue, which can be a signal or a verbal nonsense word (so you don't give the behaviour away).

- The animal must offer a series of behaviours and the trainer may select only from offered behaviours something to R+ and place under stimulus control (put the behaviour on cue).

- The trainer may use **only** a reward mark.
- The trainer uses a reward mark and a no reward mark.

Discussion after training games is very enlightening. For the first time, many people will have a look at the dog's point of view.

appendix

scheduled feeding

From a health point of view, a scheduled feed is a good idea. One of the first things your vet will ask you if you present a sick animal is "When did the dog last eat, and how much did he eat?" If you are doing free-choice feeding, you probably won't have a clue—zero help for the vet or your dog. Also, if you have multiple dogs, one bowl filled with food may be asking for trouble on several levels.

Most dogs don't get enough exercise as it is. Add to that eating out of boredom and guess what you'll have? Those of us who work with dogs see a majority of fat dogs. Yuck. All of that fat is hard to drag around and puts unnecessary strain on the dog's skeletal system, musculature, and organs.

From a training point of view, knowing when your dog is hungry is a big advantage. When Breanna had decided (after learning how to retrieve) that doing a nice retrieve was not on her job description, the rule became: If you don't get the dumbbell, you don't get dinner. The first day, I tried every 15 or 20 minutes—I would ask her to retrieve, and when she refused, I put the meal away. After about 6 of those trials, Breanna decided that retrieving was fun. To polish her drop on recall for the obedience ring, we did a drop on recall before each meal. For a moving stand, we did the same thing. This is a bit extreme, but with Breanna I have found that if I make each exercise and eating dependent upon each other, it makes a big difference in her correct response ratio.

If you have kids at home, do you play the short order cook all day, every day, on demand? Do you have meals sitting on the table all day, every day, just waiting for a time when those children *might* be interested in a meal? I bet not. We have scheduled meals for our children and for ourselves.

For many dogs, everything in life is free, free, free. Food is always available, love is always available, toys are scattered all over the floor, and so on. When your dog sees you in control of the food—the primary resource—he knows you are relevant. It's a lovely, nonconfrontational way to show him who is really in charge here. Asking Spot to work for his meal teaches your dog that the way to all of the good stuff is through obedience and you, which is just what we want Spot to think!

This is what a scheduled feed looks like:

- Divide the dog's daily ration into two portions.
- Place the first portion in a bowl.
- Feed the dog, let's say at 7:00 a.m.
- After 15 or 20 minutes, remove any unfinished portion. (If your dog has inhaled the food in 3.2 seconds, that's fine.)
- The same ritual is performed again at evening feeding time.

A feeding schedule assists you to train your dog successfully and also allows you to keep on top of his health condition.

If you are changing a dog from free-choice to a scheduled feed, expect him to perhaps not eat the portion right away. After all, he is used to having the food down all day. Stick to your guns. Within 1-5 days, you'll have a dog that understands the concept of a scheduled feed.

Obviously, if there are health considerations for your dog or you have a puppy, do what your vet and breeder recommend. Puppies between three and six months of age in my house receive three-four feedings a day. After that, two feedings per day. If your dog is fat and untrained, use portions of his daily ration of dog food to train. Also, use low-fat training treats. I will reduce my dogs' meal rations accordingly in order to accommodate healthy training treats. If you have a dog that will always go crazy for food, I say that is a trainable dog! It is so easy to get his number, because food lends itself so well to being controlled by you, the trainer.

Please use a scheduled feed for training success!

appendix

the senses

Sometimes we don't understand why our animals are displaying certain behaviours. Some of this is because we have little or no knowledge of the way they perceive the world around them. Believe me, your pet lives in a different world than the one you see and perceive. How your puppy senses the world can affect training, and the way you interpret his body language can affect the relationship and communication you have with your friend.

Dogs are social predators and scavengers. This means that they have a social structure based on cooperation within a group—pack structure, if you will. That's the social part. The predator part means that dogs will hunt and kill to eat. The scavenger part means that they will eat nearly anything (including dryer knobs if you are a Chesapeake Bay Retriever or underwire bras if you are a Labrador). Dogs are similar to humans, who were also hunter-gatherer types that coexisted in groups. To avoid aggression, dogs (as well as humans and other animals, reptiles, etc.) have an elaborate display of body language and sounds. These behaviours, which are used to express aggression, threat, fear, or appeasement to reduce or escalate conflict among the same species, are called agonistic displays. (Language, in my opinion, is one of the most fascinating and drastic adaptive traits of aggression. If something as sophisticated as language is required as part of your agonistic display, could this be an indication of just how aggressive humans are? All told, we are a pretty arrogant, destructive, and aggressive species.) Dogs have extensive display used specifically to avoid aggression and hurting each other. When dogs are in conflict with a human, they will use the same display that they would with a dog—it is all they know how to do. Humans who are unaware of what the dog is telling them are in a situation that can quickly escalate beyond control. Then, when the worst happens, the dog takes the fall. Again, I am not excusing aggression in dogs; I am asking you to educate yourself so you know how to prevent trouble.

Accepting that dogs are not "little people in fur suits" will take you a big step forward in appreciating them for the perfect creatures they are. Selective breeding for specific genetic traits has changed your dog a great deal from the wolf he once was. By studying wolf behaviour and wild or feral dog behaviour and combining that with what we know about domestic dog behaviour, a more complete picture of your dog becomes available.

I begin by thinking of all dogs as dogs and, primarily, as social predators and scavengers. This way, I can prevent many normal dog behaviours that humans consider problem behaviours from developing. It's much easier to prevent stuff than to fix it in most cases. That way if my Golden really does get along with my gerbil, I can be pleasantly surprised and take videotapes of it. I would never let my Smooths anywhere near any small animals—including cats and small, brave dogs—without extensive supervision. The results could be very sad. If you know dogs are very likely to chase things, it allows you to prevent a tragedy from happening. If it so happens that *your* dog doesn't chase everything that moves, great. But until you are absolutely certain about that particular individual's habits and breed traits, don't take any chances. In short, use common sense and caution when you are dealing with and talking to your dogs. Be even more cautious when dealing with dogs you don't know. Remember, they are dogs, and when all the chips are down, that is exactly what they will behave like.

Sight

Some breeds are more influenced by moving objects than others (for example, at the top of this list are breeds like Greyhounds, Afghans, Whippets, Border Collies, and Terriers), and this sensitivity can help and hinder your training efforts. Being careful to avoid extra or unintentional body cues can greatly speed up getting the right message across.

Dogs have more limited binocular vision compared with our own sight. That is, what dogs can see with *both* eyes at the same time is less than what we see with each of our eyes at the same time. On the other hand, because of the position of their eyes, a dog's peripheral vision far exceeds what a human is capable of. Also, as compared to human vision, the dog has different color reception and less awareness of some details. From a survival point of view, these qualities are more than compensated for by the set and position of the eyes, which gives dogs an

Sighthounds, like this Greyhound and Borzoi, are greatly influenced by moving objects. Having knowledge of your breed's natural tendencies is helpful when training.

extraordinary ability to be aware of the slightest movement over a very wide range of distance.

A study at the University of California in 1990 concluded that dogs see a similar range of colors as humans who are diagnosed as red/green color blind. That is, they distinguish around 27 hues rather than the thousands of hues in normal human color vision. Apparently, dogs see colors at one end of the spectrum, i.e., violet, blue, and indigo, while they interpret other colors as shades of yellow. Therefore, the difference between blue and red is evident, but the difference between yellow, orange, and red is not noticed.

Prevent Behaviour Problems

Dogs are easily triggered by movement. This excites their prey instinct and the desire to chase the moving object. Unfortunately, that can mean your dog is attracted to chasing bikes, cars, joggers, cats, sheep, etc. The herding breeds are notorious for this, as are terriers, though any dog can certainly display chasing behaviours. The main difference here is that you can ususally stop the herding dogs with a well-timed verbal command.

Dogs that are tied or fenced *and* unattended can display territorial aggression. Pedestrians or children moving just out of reach excite and frustrate your dog.

The frustration of being tied or confined and watching children play nearby can end up as serious trouble the day the dog gets free and vents his frustration on what he perceives as the cause of his discomfort and an outlet for all of that frustration. Those ignorant of the dog's body language, which can be the owner or the innocent bystander, can be bitten. It is my belief that as we get further and further from our rural roots, the more ignorant and intolerant the general public becomes of normal animal behaviour. I am not condoning letting dogs roam freely or giving you permission to allow your dogs to behave badly or aggressively. What I am saying is that you need to educate yourself about what dogs are really like. Don't allow dogs to make judgment calls in situations in which they cannot possibly have the background to know the right thing to do. Knowing your dog and learning how to read his body language can prevent these problems. Dogs are not likely to metamorphose into humans and do not have the means to learn spoken human language. The onus is on us to learn "dog language." We (the humans) are supposed to be the smart ones. So get smart!

Using Your Knowledge and Applying It to Training

You can teach any kind of hand signal you like. In fact, when my dogs are in tall grass, an above-the-head signal is easier for the dog to see. It is a matter of teaching the dog to respond to the cue you want to use.

Alterations to hand signals, even slight ones, tend to produce different responses. The moving hand elicits interest and action. Dogs in general react to signals more strongly and consistently than they do to the spoken voice, at least initially. Using motion as a way to get your dog's attention is very effective. Using a hand signal as a "lure" is helpful as a prompter to elicit a response when teaching your dog a verbal command. After the verbal command is learned, the hand signal may be faded out.

Jumping Up

Here is a classic case of miscommunication and the dog responding to his instincts. When Jynx jumps up and down near Abbey, snapping playfully, Abbey squeals, "No Jynx, get down" in a high-pitched voice, as she draws her hands up and slaps at Jynx, at the same time moving away from the onslaught of the excited terrier. In this scenario, common to both adults and children who are inexperienced in communicating with dogs, you are cueing and encouraging the dog to continue jumping. The high-pitched voice and motion excite the prey drive further. To Jynx, Abbey looks like a huge fun squeaky toy! The response that would obtain something closer to what you are seeking is to stand still, as motionless as you can, and ignore the behaviour. You must teach your dog to sit. This gives him an alternate behaviour. If he's sitting, he can't be jumping. When he even looks like he's going to jump, command "Sit" and don't pet him until he does. Also remember, if you allow your dog to jump on you to greet you, he will greet your guests the same way. *I* do allow my dog, Jynx, to greet me by jumping, but she also knows "Sit," and if I don't want her to jump, I make sure I command her to do so in plenty of time before she gets to me. If guests come, I instruct them to tell her to sit, or I monitor the situation carefully. The best modus operandi is to teach your dog to greet by sitting. If he gets a cookie a few times or praise, he'll soon learn to contain his excitement and sit wagging for you to pet him. Teaching your dog to sit to greet instead of punishing him will also eliminate piddling from greetings as well. Dogs submissively urinate to show respect or urinate out of excitement. Do not punish this; ignore it. Teach appropriate behaviour that you can apply R+ to. This is a good way to get rid of submissive or excitement urination. Punishing this behaviour will make it much worse.

Hearing

Dogs hear sounds in much higher frequencies than humans do. This sound sensitivity developed as a mechanism to help dogs survive in the wild. The squeaks and squawks of rodents, a potential meal, are in the ultra-sonic range.

Puppies need to practice locating sound. Knowing about their attraction to motion can entice your pup to move toward you. This handler uses a toy to attract the puppy and get his attention.

Using Your Knowledge and Applying It to Training

A high-pitched voice can elicit interest. Puppies need to practice locating sound, and knowing about their visual attraction to motion can help you to teach such commands as "Come," or to attract your dog away from something enticing outside.

Move away from Spot and use a high-pitched voice. Never run toward a dog you are calling. He either will behave defensively and run away or think you are playing tag—he being the leader—and run away. Call, clap, and move *away* from the dog or move in a lateral direction. Look interesting! If you look crabby and cross, no one wants to be near you. Why would your dog? When Spot comes, if you want to feather your nest for next time, give him social approval. Work on the speed of the recall when you have the setting events under control a little bit better.

Dogs often react to ultrasonic sounds by hyperactive behaviour and barking; we say "Be quiet—there's nothing there!" but Spot knows better.

If a previously responsive dog begins to appear to ignore commands, please have Spot's hearing checked—especially in your older friend, because the problem may be hearing loss. When detected, hearing loss is less of a problem. You can teach hand signals in order to communicate.

I got a rescue Jack Russell Terrier once. We called her Daisy and she was adorable. The owners told me that "she just doesn't listen!" Almost every rescue terrier I have taken in has been accompanied by this remark. This is hardly a rare occurrence for a terrier. The original owners had obtained the dog as a puppy, and she was four years old when I got her. She was *way* too much dog for their family, and while they were kind, they were also very relieved that I would take the dog. It was during a very busy summer at my boarding kennel, so I sort of "stored" her until I could start to work with her. She was a very adaptable and happy little dog and soon learned the kennel routine from the kennel "regulars" that she went outside with. She watched them and did whatever they did and got cookies for being a good girl. She was a barker, but that is not unusual in a terrier. She also didn't come when called, but that is also not out of the realm of normal behaviour in rescue dogs that I get. I had her about three months before I was able to fiddle with her training. Daisy was a very quick study; she picked up on the hand signals and the whole "training game" thing rapidly. Then came that time in training when I was moving her sit and down on to a verbal cue. She was so bright that it surprised me when she just didn't seem to get it. You are by now thinking what a dimwit I am, right?! After a couple of days of trying to get this verbal cue thing to sink in, it finally dawned on me that Daisy really *didn't* listen!

No wonder she had no recall, no wonder I couldn't "talk" to her. Once this finally occurred to me, I began watching her very closely, and sure enough, unless she felt a vibration, she did not respond to sound. You could slap two pans together behind her and she didn't even flinch a bit. Daisy was eventually placed with a loving family who accepts the responsibility for keeping a deaf dog safe. What an unusually intelligent animal! Daisy was able to adapt so astutely to life that she had everyone fooled. But what a tragedy it could have been had I not discovered she was deaf. I don't like to think about the punishment she probably endured at one time or another because "she wouldn't listen."

Smell

Dogs have an incredible sense of smell. Trying to explain how vividly the nose of a dog transmits smells to their brain would be like trying to explain sight to a person who had been blind from birth. A theoretical example of this would be if a gram of butyric acid were made to evaporate evenly in all the rooms of a ten-story office building, a man would barely be able to perceive its existence by standing in one of the rooms. However, if the same gram was diluted to fill the air above the entire city of Hamburg, a dog could still perceive it at an altitude of

Dogs have an incredible sense of smell, which can aid you when training them for certain jobs, such as tracking. Here Maeve, the German Shepherd, has learned to lie down to indicate that she has found an article dropped on the track.

300 feet (derived from *Scent and the Scenting Dog*, by William G. Syrotuck, 1972, Arner Publications).

Dogs have been used by humans for centuries because of their acute sense of smell and aptitude at locating animals, items, and people by tracking, trailing, and in the case of some sporting breeds, flushing and pointing game—sport today, but survival to our ancestors.

A dog's sense of smell can be an asset and a nuisance, and even dangerous in a domestic environment. Some poisons, i.e., rat and snail bait, smell very attractive to a dog but can kill him. Antifreeze is another deadly substance dogs love. Those chocolates wrapped gaily and placed under the Christmas tree—you don't know they're yummy yet, but Spot does after he sniffs them out! Chocolate can be poisonous to dogs, so don't feed them chocolate or place chocolates where your dog can reach them and help himself to them. The smell of food from the counter can encourage "stealing." Rubbish bins are just like ambrosia to your dog.

Dogs are attracted to smells and substances we find distasteful and disgusting. Fresh horse manure, cat feces, carrion, etc. are all olfactory delights to Spot. Some naturalists believe that wild dogs and wolves are attempting to disguise their own odor so the animals they prey upon do not detect them so quickly. Others believe that it is like humans using perfume. Whatever the case, I know my own little pals love to roll in revolting things, then joyfully run to me to share this wonderful experience, dancing around me gaily as I gag. Dogs will be dogs. The only help for this is a bath—after which, of course, I'm relieved and my dog is disgusted!

Using Your Knowledge and Applying It to Training

Because dogs are so sensitive to scent, don't be surprised when smells are extremely distracting to Spot, particularly with the scenthounds that can hardly bear to lift their heads up off the ground.

Keep your dog safe from hazards that could kill him. Antifreeze, wrapped chocolates, or other foods—these can be dangerous for an innocent little sniffer.

Touch

People stroke and pat their dogs to enjoy the pleasure that stroking a fuzzy buddy brings and also to show love and affection. People undeniably love to pet their pets, but do our dogs see it the same way?

Most dogs do enjoy physical contact. However, if you watch dogs being dogs or wolves in their environment, you will see that canines do not necessarily use touch to show emotion and approval as extensively as humans do. Grooming

Touch can be an important way to communicate with your dog, and your dog should learn to accept your care and handling happily.

behaviours among the same species can mean many things. Grooming can be a bonding behaviour—something you do for each other because it heightens a family feeling. Dogs groom each other because it is stress-relieving and relaxing for both the groomer and the one being groomed. Grooming can be a ranking behaviour—the dominant dog is allowed to groom the subordinate dog for as long as he likes, whenever he likes. Submissive members are allowed to groom higher ranking members after obtaining permission. When Punch was small, she used to love to sprawl on Fletcher, my Basset Hound. He adored her also and they spent many lazy hours together. As Punch reached adulthood, she would growl if Fletcher moved to get up and make him wait until *she* wanted to move. Punch also likes to clean Fletcher's face and will also growl if he tries to move away. He stands there and takes it. Rank is an interesting phenomenon in dog packs. Like in human groups, rank is liquid. Fletch may hold still for grooming and lounging, but God help the unfortunate one who tries to remove toys from his cavernous jaws. Punch and the other terriers know when to back off.

Dogs frequently lick our faces; this is a greeting behaviour, identifiable in young puppies with their mother or other caregivers. It encourages regurgitation of a yummy meal from elder to pup.

Dogs may also lick hands, etc. This is classified as "care-seeking" behaviour if you are talking to an ethologist. If you only allow licking occasionally, give a command or signal to allow a "kiss." If you do not like it at all, discourage the behaviour with a "No" in a neutral tone and pointedly ignore your dog. Your dog will soon invent alternative methods of care-seeking. With any luck at all, the new methods will not be more annoying than the licking behaviour.

Using Your Knowledge and Applying It to Training

Touch can be perceived as threatening to dogs, even if not intended so by the human involved, particularly, touching the top or back of the head or the top of the neck or shoulders. These are areas dogs use with each other to pull rank. Other extremely "touch sensitive" areas are the hindquarters and anal face.

Food is preferred by many dogs over touch when training. This is not to affront you personally. It doesn't mean that your dog doesn't love you and doesn't want to be touched. Sometimes I, myself, prefer food and other times hugs and kisses are what I am looking for. This is not surprising when you break everything down to the lowest common denominator. I am not discounting touch here as a necessity; we know it is essential to nurturing and development. It is well documented that baby creatures that do not receive the proper kind of nurturing (including touch) do not grow up to be normal representatives of their species. But, relatively speaking, you can live without being touched longer than you can live without food.

Many trainers and books advise hitting with newspapers, kneeing Spot in the chest, pulling his ears, or harsh

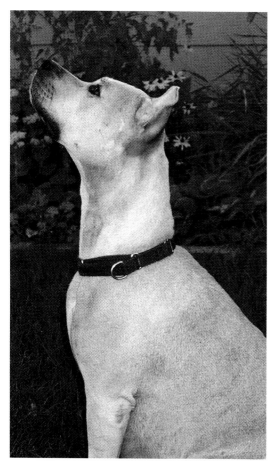

Martingale or controlled slip collars are superior to choke or slip collars because they prevent the dog from slipping out without choking him.

repeated corrections with slip collars. These methods, particularly if incorrectly timed, can lead to fear, resentment, avoidance, and stress for your friend. None of these are conditions conducive to learning a wanted or alternative behaviour. Some of these methods, such as ear pulling, can physically harm and damage your dog. Slip collars, used incorrectly, can damage the trachea permanently. There are many alternatives to teaching your dog how to behave without yelling, jerking, or choking—which can permanently injure your dog. If you are concerned about your dog backing out of a flat collar, get a limited slip-type collar or a Martingale collar. You can adjust the amount of "slip" on these kinds of collars. This prevents the dog from backing out of the collar, but will not continue to tighten and choke the dog. Now, go out there and appreciate your dog for the wonderful perfect being he is!

appendix

what does your dog like?

Choosing Reinforcers for Training

This list will provide you with primary reinforcers and many other options for secondary reinforcers (this idea came from John Rogerson's book). It is a great help for making students more aware of their dog's likes and dislikes. Life rewards are very salient and make excellent alternatives for reinforcers. You must use a variety of R+ to best maintain behaviour.

Use this list as a reference from which to choose R+ for your dog. Please note that we don't care what your preferences are currently. Maybe we will later on, but for now, look at life through your dog's eyes—what does he like? What does he beg to do? What does he beg to eat? What is he doing when he looks happy and relaxed? Contented? What activities does he avoid? When you are touching him, for which touches does he look like he'd rather be somewhere else?

List your dog's favorite items to play with in order of preference.

1.   2.   3.

List activities that your dog would rather do than anything else in the world. List the most favored first.

1.   2.   3.

List the kind of physical contact your dog enjoys the most. List in order of preference.

Petting   Cuddling   Stroking
Tickling   Scratching   Playful Shoving

If you asked your dog what he wanted to do today and where he wanted to go, what would he say?

1.   2.   3.

How does your dog get your attention when he wants it?

1.   2.   3.

List your dog's favorite foods.

1.   2.   3.

involvement or "for your eyes only"

This work is applicable for every dog/handler team. If you don't have attention, you don't have anything! If you are not *giving* as well as receiving attention, you don't have teamwork.

Eye contact should be an invitation for your dog to "come on in." I prefer the word **involvement** to the terms commonly used here, like attention or focus. Involvement implies that there is a team effort and that the communication loop is open. (Chris Bach is responsible for validating much of my thinking with this. I had been using a lot of "leave it" type exercises to get the dog to look away from the food and to look at my face. But her seminar put the polish on this exercise for me and added that smack of sophistication I was looking for. So thank you Chris for clarifying a couple of points for me. Success is in the details!)

This work is also of great benefit to pet owners. In my pet classes, we do involvement work. In fact, that is what I begin all of my classes with. For those going on to do competition, we get serious about involvement work and do frequent quick reviews throughout the dog's career.

Before you begin, remember that it is normal for your dog to react to something sudden that startles him. He will probably always glance toward whatever startled him, but it should be a glance, not a change of involvement from you to the distraction. I look at the recovery time—how long did the dog look at the distraction? If your dog says "Hey! What's that?!" with a glance, that situation would be pretty unavoidable. If your dog says, "Oh! Cool!" and begins to move toward the distraction, you may try the following strategies to regain his involvement with you:

- Move into the dog, carefully, but at the same time try to surprise him.
- Move between the dog and the distraction.
- Keep the motion up, with frequent changes of direction until the dog attends to you.
- Move away from the distraction, until the dog looks at you.
- If the dog moves away from you, move away from him, too. He will be attracted by the motion and follow.

I do not use leash corrections or verbal corrections implying disfavor or disgust. Nagging and other verbal chatter tends to make the dog's eyes glaze over and soon he is looking everywhere but at you. *You* are a boring nag. I wouldn't look either. This is because punishment of that ilk makes for very excellent discrimination skills and the apparent irritation here is you. Therefore, you become the item to avoid, putting the team into obvious conflict of interest. Have you ever gotten a speeding ticket? So you *never*, ever did that again, right? Or did you just get more discriminating: Speeding is safe if there are no cops around?

The strategies listed above help the dog become attracted to you, rather than repelled by you. Using harsher aversives than listed is like using a serrated steak knife to do surgery. You may still get the job done, but the elegance factor is way down. The wear and tear factor on your dog and the relationship is way up.

Prepare and Plan

Begin training in a distraction-free environment where your dog feels safe. You will need a treat that can be swallowed in one gulp—no chewing (by the dog) and one that can be put in your mouth if you choose to go that route. Especially for those doing competition type work, your mouth is a great place to store food. It looks like you don't have any food (not obviously in your hands or in a fanny pack, etc.). Also, getting your dog to watch your face is easy if you spit food at him. Spot will keep a close eye on where that food is coming from!

Pick a word that means "you are to give me your attention." (Look, watch, ready are some suggestions, or you can use your dog's name. Or you can do what I do and use a couple of attention words. Caution: Please have the word ready for use, but **do not** use the word until you have the behaviour! Otherwise you get missed associations.) Your cue of "Ready" is not so much "Watch me!" as it is a predictor of R+. "Ready" is understood to mean that opportunities for R+ are now available. Do not underestimate the power of opportunity for reinforcement. It takes us all to work every day, even when the weather is bad or you have a cold. You will also need a release signal, so your dog knows when he is working. The terminal response (end goal) is stimulus control. Stimulus control implies that I can begin and end the behaviour on cue.

Remember: Baby steps, baby steps, baby steps to success.

Manufacture

You can begin with reinforcing all of the attention your dog gives you voluntarily. Where you begin with each dog will depend somewhat on the individual dog and how much he seeks to interact with you naturally, giving up what the environment itself has to offer. If the dog seeks out my company, a lot of social interaction and treats are in order. For a very self-sufficient dog (read: not always interested in what you're doing), you may begin by applying R+ ("Yes" and a treat) to the behaviour of just being near you and hanging around.

Here are some moves to try: Move backward or laterally away from the dog. Apply R+ (RM and a cookie) to moving toward you or staying near you.

Baby Step #1: Eye Contact

What your dog is probably really looking at and paying attention to at this point in the training is the food. We are now going to fix that. Stand with your arms at your sides. Your dog may nudge, paw, look at the hand with the food, and leap. Remain neutral and still. Wait. The dog may bark. If the dog tries to leave,

Reinforce the attention that your dog gives to you by providing an RM and a treat when he focuses on you. Here, the handler gets down on the dog's level to make it easier for the dog to direct his attention to the handler's face.

step on the long line or leash and don't allow that behaviour. However, put up with everything else. Ignore it all. Suddenly, in frustration, the dog will glance up at your face. Mark it and feed it. The dog must be looking up to get the treat. Initially, I will reward even very short glances. Then I will ask for two glances, and then a stare before I will deliver the RM and the primary. In this manner, I can begin to harden the dog's resolve to keep working and pay attention, even at this early stage. This work can be done with very young puppies at 7 or 8 weeks of age if you take their gnat-like attention span into account.

This is a bit of a patience game, but I want the dog to voluntarily look at me. I am not going to prompt, remind, help, or any of that stuff. It is time for the dog "to do his own homework." You cannot do it for him. Patience, Prudence. Allow your dog to problem solve!

Whether the dog is sitting, standing, or lying down does not matter. I am initially looking for eye contact. At first, just glances are fine. Then I seek to prolong the eye contact and want the dog to commit to gazing into my eyes—not my chin or ears, but looking into my eyes with the intensity that indicates that he is making a conscious decision to commit to using my eyes as a target for his eye

Small dogs may also be placed on a table to raise them. This way, the handler doesn't have to bend and the dog's options are limited. It also helps the dog to focus.

contact. I want my dog to accept my invitation to "come on in." Now we can have a chat over tea!

Baby Step #2: R+ Eye Contact

R+ eye contact. Stop R+ "swipes" and look for that commitment your dog makes to look into your eyes for longer and longer periods of time. If you release the dog with the release signal ("All done," or whatever command you are using) and the dog chooses to continue working with you, I would certainly R+ that. The dog must be calm and still in order to maintain eye contact. As a by-product, you are reinforcing this calm and involved behaviour.

At this point you have a dog that is receiving a treat around every 3-5 seconds. Work that up to around 20 or more seconds.

Baby Step #3: Adding the Cue

Now that you have a lot of voluntary involvement (attention, including eye contact), you may think about adding the cue. When you have attention that is past the glance and is approaching 10-20 seconds of intense eye contact, you may begin using your watch word. (Add the verbal cue.) However, you must give the dog a release signal before the eye contact goes away. Otherwise, you are teaching the dog that there is no clear time when to work and when not to work. This is very confusing for the dog. So, at first you must release the dog *before* he looks away. As you increase criteria, you will wait longer and longer before giving the release signal. Bringing a behaviour under stimulus control dictates that we have the behaviour to begin with. Be careful adding that cue! Adding a cue too soon always results in problems later. The more reliable the behaviour and the closer it is to the terminal response before you add the cue, the better the end result and performance will be. "Look," "Watch," "Ready"—all of these are good words to use. I use "Look" and "Ready." If you say, "Ready," and the dog looks at you and is fed a treat, pretty soon you'll say, "Ready," and he will be looking up into your eyes on cue. Looking at you becomes a very big predictor of R+. We are all constantly searching out opportunities for reinforcement. We want eye contact to become such a predictor of R+ that soon it becomes a habit—involvement from your dog as a habit! I'll take that; it's so much better than many other behaviour options my dog has.

Baby Step #4: Voluntary Attention

Next, show the dog the food and hold it out, but not near your face. Don't lure the dog into looking at your face more than three or four times. Luring is a last resort. Holding the food out to your side at arm's length is a good place to begin. Show the dog the food in your hand, then move the hand out at arm's length. The dog will have to make a decision that is very obvious to you about what he is going to look at. You may be kneeling on the floor or standing. If you choose to begin with kneeling, you are adding an additional step, which may be applicable for some dogs. You may also choose to have your small dog up on a grooming table; then move him to the floor. Wait quietly (no chattering—we want the dog to problem solve.) When he

Adding a verbal cue and a hand signal will assist your dog in directing his attention toward you.

figures out for himself that eye contact is not only his very own original idea, but also yields treat, he will be hooked.

My intention here is that I see the dog making a conscious decision to look *away* from the food magnet and look at *me*. This teaches the dog many things. Direct access to goodies is not the straight line it seems to be. The line travels from the dog through the handler, and the handler provides the goodies. If I can get my dog to buy into the fact that goodies are available through his calm and focused behaviour, I have made a great step forward in "the big R" (our relationship), as well a giant step forward in compliance and deference to my requests.

I am looking for voluntary attention. I do not wish to prompt or nag my dog into paying attention. As a matter of fact, when you release most dogs, they beg to come back and work for more. (R+ that!) My dogs want to work. Work is the best predictor of reinforcement that they have.

Baby Step #5: Use the Sit

A dog that is in a sitting position in front of you is easiest for most handler/dog teams. You may have to put the dog in a sit and work your way into a front position using R+. This is fine. Other dogs will just end up sitting in front of you because it is the easiest place to play this game. Most dogs sitting out in front of you are too far away to be correct for the competition ring. Now it is time to teach the dog to come closely into your space and that it is safe. Many dogs are made uneasy by people leaning over them. It has nothing to do with rank and everything to do with an individual's need to maintain a certain "personal space."

Think about personal space for a moment. You are in a crowded elevator. The elevator stops and another person enters. Because there are so many people on the elevator, this stranger squishes in and stands right next to you. Because of the crowded conditions, this person's shoulder and arm are touching your shoulder and arm. (Pretty normal situation.) Think how differently you might feel in the following scenario: You are the only person on an elevator and the elevator stops. Another person enters the elevator. This stranger enters and the door closes. The stranger moves so he is standing so close his body is touching yours. Oooh! I can feel the hair rise on the back of my neck just thinking about it. There are social conventions that can have an effect on personal space, as illustrated above. Your dog may not be aware of those because of a lack of education or he may be fearful because of past experiences.

Another option to use if the dog is not looking at you is to say the dog's name to

get his attention. Bring your left hand down and show the food, then hide the food or hold the food out like you did before. Wait for that all-important eye contact to occur voluntarily. Then wait for the dog to commit. Please do this prompting as little as possible, if you do it at all. You are much better off waiting it out and letting the dog figure it out. No treat is given if the dog is not looking at you. If you have to prompt more than once, you need to go back and do a review session (review the first steps again with your dog to remind him what the appropriate behaviour is).

In the very beginning, encourage your dog to look at your face by showing him a treat and holding it near your nose.

Baby Step #6: Introduce Premack

Put eye contact into every context. Ask Spot "Do you want out of your crate? Do you want to go outside, get dinner, be on the sofa, be on my lap, get pats or scratches, etc.? Give me involvement first, then you can have it." This makes the game relevant to everyday life for your dog. If he is looking at you, he is learning to ask permission and looks to you for input about his behaviour.

I want my dog's belief system to become: "I get the best of the environment by going through my partner." This encourages your dog to literally see a distraction and instead of going to it, he will look at you for input. Through classical conditioning and associative learning, the distraction becomes an antecedent cue to involve himself with you.

Baby Step #7: Use An NRM

Non-attention can result in a no reward mark (NRM) now. Most of my students are ready to do this after 5-10 attention sessions. A session would consist of probably 3-10 trials. A trial would begin with "Ready" and end with your release command. The goal of each session is to add 2-5 seconds to the dog's attention span; therefore taking him out of the "gnat class" and into a realm where 15 seconds of attention is feasible.

Big important note: If I have to use an NRM, I am going to assume that I need to do some more homework. After all, I don't want to use an NRM to get attention—I want that attention voluntarily. So if you are compelled to use an NRM more than once, instead shut your mouth and back up before you say "too bad." At this juncture I would go back to the earlier sequences and review the material with my dog. I am not going to correct for non-attention, but I will make sure the dog understands the material well.

Baby Step #8: Pivot From Heel to Front

Your dog is sitting and you step into heel position. The leash is under your foot if your dog has a tendency to wander or needs to be kept safe. Have treats in your left hand. Once you have the dog's attention, say "Stay." Holding food in line with the dog's face, slowly pivot to the front. If his attention wavers while you are pivoting, freeze. Wait. Be patient. When the dog looks back at you, mark it, feed him, and continue the pivot. Think in terms of: "We are doing this together." Initially, when you are conditioning the attention, wait for the dog and keep applying R+ to the attention you get. You'll get more. That's one of the rules. Whatever is R+ed will be repeated.

During the exercise, the dog's head should stay tilted toward you if he is sitting in heel position. If your dog is in front of you, he should have his head up. Taller dogs will be able to look at your face without backing up. For very short dogs, looking at your waist is good. Otherwise, the dog has to sort of back up or roll back on his haunches to see your eyes. A Dachshund may have to look at your knees. Take a look and make a judgment call—Is the dog paying attention? If so, mark it and feed him. If not, you can wait patiently because your dog will look at you sooner or later. You may also try getting his attention initially—move away, make kissy noises, move your hand briefly, etc.

Baby Step #9: Heel Position

Put the leash under your foot or keep it off and have treats in your left hand. Once you have the dog's attention , request a sit. Next, step into heel position. Use your body posture as a cue for "Heel" and to offer attention to you. If the dog's attention is still on you, say, "Ready" or "Heel," and give him a treat. (I use both words for associative learning purposes.) Feed your dog so that the treat is placed where you want his visual reference point to be for heeling. For most dogs, this will be somewhere on your legs or on your pant leg seam, the height varying considerably depending on the height of your dog. Reinforcement placement is important to your finished product. Begin to wait longer and longer between the "Ready" and/or the RM and delivery of the food.

When teaching the heel, move into position beside your dog. Move your hand up in gradual degrees to help your dog understand the final heel cue and the desired behaviour.

Your dog will depend very much on your body language, as well as your verbal cue to indicate when to give intense attention, such as we are asking for here. You cannot rely on food to train your dog. R+ training is all about developing a relationship between you and your dog. After you release, take a mental break or play break and then begin another trial. Do 3-5 trials maximum per session. You can do 2 or 3 sessions a day if you like. Whenever you have a minute!

As soon as possible you are standing, not kneeling, with your small dogs. Dogs who were started on a table are now moved to the floor.

Baby Step #10: Formal Postures

Just so you are doing this as a separate exercise and are aware of the importance of it, pair the eye contact exercises with your formal ring postures of front and heel. If you have been doing this correctly, this has been evolving in a very natural way. Now you want to double check your formal postures in a mirror. With fronts, you are probably looking at your dog. However, in heel you are probably (or should be) watching where you are going, so with your dog sitting in heel, look out ahead of you as if you were walking and R+ your dog for remaining in heel position.

Baby Step #11: Challenges

You need to prepare your dog for being dependable about remaining involved with you. You are not trying to see if you can get the dog to mess up—the distraction is used to help build his confidence and to clarify the exercise for the dog.

You are starting to ask the dog to look at you longer in order to get the treat. You are no longer giving a constant feed under rehearsed contexts, but when you first add distractions you might need to go back to kindergarten temporarily. Warning: People usually go wrong in this sequence and make training errors by having their criteria too high or too low for the dog's current skill level.

- Dog looks at the distraction.
- Dog looks back at you. Count to 3 (or make sure the dog is committed).
- RM the behaviour.
- Give the dog the treat.

Challenge List

- Toss or drop a piece of food (please pay attention—step on food or move away if the dog goes for or looks at the food).
- Have someone else walk by and toss food.
- Have a person walk around the dog at a distance of 10 to 15 feet.
- Have a person talk while walking the dog.
- Have a person get closer to the dog, gradually.
- Have a person bounce a ball or carry an umbrella that they swing gently.
- Have a person offer the dog food.
- Repeat the above with pivot to front.

Postscript: As an alternative to the NRM, you can take off at a dead run. That begins to surprise Spot, and he will try harder to keep track of you! If you have to do this more than one time, move right into doing a review session. A review session consists of going back to earlier sequences and going through them with your dog to remind him the correct way to do the exercise. For instance, go back to holding food out at arm's length and getting eye contact, etc.

Baby Step #12: Challenges From Heel and Front

Begin with no food in hand, but have treats in your mouth or located on a table or in a training bag. This way you can store food on you or near you without begin obvious about it.

The handler is to become more and more quiet for longer periods of time, giving the dog less frequent feedback. This will harden the dog's resolve to hang in there and continue to pay attention, even though it may be more difficult to do so.

Assume handler position at heel or front. The person now comes up to the dog and strokes him. If the dog looks away, NRM. If you need to NRM more than once, go to a review session. You may have to begin again with a constant feed, gradually hardening the dog's resolve to resist the distraction and win the prize.

Do your challenges from a heel or front position (make sure to practice both).

Once your dog is paying attention to you automatically and consistently, you can challenge him and be ready to review if he breaks his concentration.

Also work backwards, one step at a time, until you are six feet away and return to the heel position before releasing.

Challenge List

A person comes up to the dog, strokes him, and tells him to lie down. Do not use the dog's name or a strict voice, but a soft or neutral voice. Have the helper be very subtle. The second the dog begins to respond to the distraction, your helper must cease attention immediately and pointedly ignore the dog. Initially, you may want to do this in steps:

•Provide a constant feed for the dog as the helper lightly

touches him.

- The helper touches the dog and if he resists distraction, then provide the RM and a treat.
- If the dog loses attention or goes down, NRM.
- Wait for the dog's attention to come back to you and then begin another trial.

Baby Step #13: Practice

You have a lot of automatic attention by this time. Now begin heeling starts. Say, "Ready." With both feet still together, just barely lean forward as you sort of naturally do to begin walking. Take one step and give the dog a cookie.

Around week five of training, we also teach the dogs to begin with moving in heel. A good attention-getter is to use a little tap right in the center of the top of the head. Go easy—this is a tiny tap indicating, "Where are you?" You could also run off in the opposite direction, and when the dog catches up with you, wait to receive 3-5 seconds or more of attention and then mark it and feed it. If you have to prompt for attention, it is time for a review session! Do it right now; don't wait until tomorrow. Lack of attention necessitates going back and doing a quick review for the dog and utilizing the first steps you used to get his attention—that is, holding out food at arm's length and dropping food while the dog maintains attention and/or eye contact.

Now work on the sit. If the dog looks away during the sit, even if he is looking back at you, he is making a choice. Be patient and wait for the dog. If I am getting no attention, I might try crating the dog for 5 minutes. My attitude is: "If you won't play with me, you don't get to play at all." If you choose to do any correction at all—like moving away from whatever is currently distracting the dog—the dog will turn after the correction to locate you and must see you looking like a fun playmate, with a ball or a treat in your hand and wearing a big smile.

IMPORTANT! The biggest mistake you can make is to correct Spot or to frown when Spot is looking at you. Why? Think about it! Obviously, this would be applying an aversive to the desired behaviour. This is a big mistake! The term "correction" may also need a bit of clarification here so we don't have a war over semantics. Correction to me is *not* a leash correction. Most often it is removing my person (therefore, opportunities for reinforcement go way down) or, if the dog is on leash, moving in the opposite direction of the distraction so distance can diminish the value of one reinforcer while enhancing my own reinforcement value.

If your dog looks at you but is obviously dreaming of a vacation on the beach in Bali, tap his head and then do a review session.

Secrets of Success

Timing is all important here. Enthusiasm is a must. Please use body postures that the dog will eventually see in the show ring and look pleasant. Don't forget to smile!

Working with mirrors can be very helpful. Many of the formal postures used in the ring do not include gazing into the dog's eyes. Each one of these postures must be introduced to the dog and plied with R+. Otherwise the dog may become nervous in the ring, because your cues look different. If the cue is different than the one the dog has seen in training, it is certainly not his fault if he doesn't have a clue in the ring. Wake up and smell the coffee, folks. Pay attention to your body language.

For those doing competition work: From this point forward, when you ask the dog to sit, pay attention and don't be gazing around yourself. Get in there, get the involvement, do the exercise, and then give a clear release signal. The minute the dog is in heel position, it is time to go to work and attention is a must. If you have the dog in heel position, you must be as involved as you want your dog to be. It is not fair to keep the dog in heel position if *you* are not paying attention.

Give the dog a piece of food that he can see. If the food is dropped by accident and I cannot prevent the dog from getting the treat, I tell the dog, "Get it." If you do not tell the dog to "Get it," you must prevent him from getting it. Step on it or move away. Learning to hoover the floor is not what you are teaching him. It's not the end of the world if you don't drop your treats *all* the time. With practice you will develop enough dexterity not to drop them.

Do this 2 times a day for up to 3, 4, or 5 trials.

Keep the vision!

Checklist

Manufacture Attention R+ Glances	Dates:	Notes:
Stop R+ Swipes—Look for more commitment		
Dog must make a choice—look at food held out at arm's length or engage in eye contact		
Intro eye contact as a way to access Premack behaviours		
Add verbal cue		
Pair involvement with formal ring postures: Front and heel		
Add challenges to front		
Add challenges to heel		

no! not the "p" word !

It is unfortunate that to be a good dog trainer you must be a bit detail-oriented. That nasty old word, "planning," must play a part in any training program. In fact, you have to allow planning to get right up on that stage with you.

I don't want to hear any grumbling, now. There is no one that can hold a candle to me in the area of disorganization. My entire life is always lost in a shambles of chaos and dirty laundry wherever I go. Leaving the house is always a comedy. I get in the van, begin to pull down the drive, back up at full speed, belt into the

If you want a well-educated dog, you must plan ahead for each training session. Here, Breeze, owned by Mary Wilmoth, catches up on his reading before class.

house, and run in to get an item that I've forgotten. My husband looks up from the paper and says goodbye again. In a few seconds I realize that I've forgotten something else or come back in for some other item because I didn't actually get the item I went into the house for in the first place. As I leave the house the second time, my husband says, "Trip #2 and counting." He thinks he is so clever. I read books with titles like *Organization for the Creative Among Us.* Books like these are wonderful. One of the books I read talked about how creative people don't like to put things out of sight in closets or in drawers because they lose them. I nodded my head in agreement as I read this; yes, yes, someone understands me! Creative nature was discussed throughout the whole book. Despite reading it, I am still extremely disorganized, but I feel really good about that now.

Organizing for dog training is more fun than housework—that's a big plus. It's even more fun than going to the dentist.

Get a training bag. Put the items you'll need to train your dog in it. I tend to get carried away and end up with an entire mini-van full of junk just to train one 18-pound dog, but here is a list you can begin with.

Training Bag

- Fanny pack or bait bag to carry food in
- Tupperware containers to carry extra food in
- Training notebook
- Balls, fuzzy mice, squeaky toys, flying disks
- Baby wipes to wash your hands with when there is no water available
- Clickers (if you use them)
- Stopwatch (to time sits and downs accurately)
- Extra leash and collar (over the years I've been grateful for this more than once!)
- Water bowl and water for the dog (save a soda bottle to put travel water in)
- Extra bones for your dog chew on while you are socializing with your training buddies (if you don't start out with one, you may meet one at the park where you are generalizing all those behaviours)

For those of you who do competition work, add the following:
- Ruler for your jumps
- Jumps
- Dumbbell
- Obedience rule books

Before you can teach a behaviour, you have to know what you're going to do about the following:

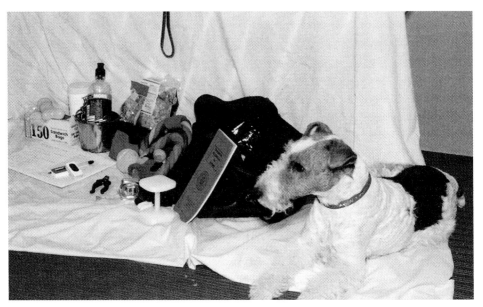

Here is an example of a well-stocked training bag: an extra collar and leash; plastic bags for cleaning up after your dog; a bone and toys; a bottle of water and a drinking bowl; baby wipes for cleaning up after you; a pen and your training plan; a bait bag and goodies; a clicker; a stopwatch and measuring tape; nail clippers; and the Obedience regulations, dumbbell, and gloves.

A = Antecedent

How are you going to elicit the behaviour?

What is your cue (antecedent) going to be?

Can you deliver your antecedent in a consistent manner?

B = Behaviour

What is the target behaviour (the behaviour you want to work on)?

What is the terminal response? (The finished behaviour. You may not get that today because you are probably working on shaping or chaining your way toward this.)

What are you shaping today? Choose one behaviour at a time to work on. Relax requirements for other steps initially. Frequency, duration, intensity.

What will you reinforce?

C = Consequence

Reinforcers: Primary / RM / Premack behaviours

No reward mark

Schedule — Fixed / Variable

You can use a flowchart to help plan your training of behaviours. It helps you to see where you need work, but best of all it indicates your progress and keeps you organized–even if you're like me.

Plan your own schedule!

My planning ladders include the following information:

Ladder for behaviour: _____

Dog's name: _____**Date:** _____

Describe terminal response (end goal). You have to know where you're going in order to get there!:

Final cues used to elicit behaviour—No special conditions required!:

Prompts that will be used in training. Everybody needs a little help sometime!:

Successive Approximations

Begin with the antecedent.

Take a look at the behaviour.

Provide appropriate consequences.

You can copy and use this ladder to plan your own behaviour topography.

Ladder for behaviour: _____

Dog's name: _____**Date:** _____

Describe terminal response (end goal). You have to know where you're going in order to get there!:

Antecedent: Final cues used to elicit behaviour—no special conditions required!

Antecedent (temporary): Prompts that will be used in training. Everybody needs a little help sometime!:

Successive Approximations:

Target Behaviour	Consequence	Reinforcement Schedule	Remarks & Date	# of Trials

(Here is a little example. I took this from my training notes.)

My planning ladders include the following information:

Ladder for behaviour: Retrieve over a high jump

Dog's name: Breanna   **Date:** 5/29/96

Describe terminal response (end goal). You have to know where you're going in order to get there!:

AKC High Jump Dog in heel, throw dumbbell, send dog over jump, dog jumps and retrieves, dog presents & holds dumbbell, dog relinquishes dumbbell, dog finishes.

Final cues used to elicit behaviour—No special conditions required!:

Stay command and signal, (verbal "Stay" with right hand signal, dumbbell in left hand) verbal only "Bree take", verbal only "Thank you," hand signal only to finish.

Prompts that will be used in training. Everybody needs a little help sometime!:

Lures, hand gestures, play behaviours for retrieving and jumping, verbals.

Successive Approximations:

Target Behaviour	Consequence	Reinforcement Schedule	Remarks & Date # of Trials
Follow steps for carefully for inducive retrieve		Retrieve is on variable schedule	Okay at this date
Front with dumbbell is intact		On variable schedule	Okay at this date
Practice jumping all kinds of jumps—Go with the dog, have her go over without me. Work from left and right	RM, Food, other auxiliary R+, or NRM, follow up with help	On variable schedule	5/24/96 lots of x's used bar, solid, series, pieces of paper laying on the ground, people
Recall over jumps	As above	On variable schedule	As of 5/24/96
Dog in sit stay with DB other side of jump. Recall over low (8") jump	As above	On fixed schedule No fronts yet Added fronts, FRI, 6/1/96 1x	5/24/96 3x's 5/28/96 2x's 5/30/96 4x's

Successive Approximations:

Target Behaviour	Consequence	Reinforcement Schedule	Remarks & Date # of Trials
Fun retrieves over jump, help getting back	As above Prompt: tap mid of jump to focus dog and call her as she picks up db and turns.	On fixed schedule	5/20/96 3x's 5/23/96 4x's 6/3/96 1x
Place DB at an angle, lots of help	As above	Fixed schedule, prompts	6/3/96
Add fronts to "angle" retrieve	Chutes, maybe? No physical prompts	FRI - no finish. Chutes worked good	6/8/96 (2x's)
Add sit Stay in heel Toss DB. R+ stay	R+, physical restraint if required		
Add finish to all the above			
Ring Procedure			
Raise jump height to 10", then 12", etc. to full height Do lots of fun stuff also			

Proofing:

Different surfaces, yes 6/3/96

Different locations 5/28/96 class; 5/24 Currie Park; 6/3 Tridge

Noise using dog show tape frequently

Someone moving around us 5/28 class

Someone doing a retrieve nearby 6/1 dropped into a class

Toys scattered

Long grass-blind retreive

6/3/96: Trouble going around high jump on return–I have effectively patterned her to go around the 1st trial and come back over the 2nd trial. Now what? Duh/checking.

6/4/96: Decided to put high jump in a chute—worked great. We'll stay in the chute for 20 trials, then try without the chute and see where we are. Practice throwing dumbell without the dog.

the perfect sit/stay

Goals

The dog will sit on command.

He will stay until released.

Concepts for the Dog to Understand

Length of time to stay.

Distance.

Resisting distraction.

Crash Course on Learning Theory as it Applies to the Sit

You will initially use a primary reinforcer (food) to elicit the behaviour in the form of a "lure." You will also use the food to associate a specific word with meaning, like "That's it!" This word is your reward mark. The words "Yes" or "Good" work well as a reward mark. A reward mark becomes very meaningful to your dog as it gives him information. Concise communication is the name of the game.

The perfect sit/stay consists of the dog sitting on command and staying until he is released.

You will use a no reward mark, such as "Too bad" or "Try again" to signal to the dog that you don't want the behaviour he is currently offering. Do *not* deliver the food treat. Do not use the word "No," because it is probably already overused in communication between you and your pet.

Initially, the food treat is offered *every time* the sit is accomplished. At the point that you can bet me 10 bags of dog food that the dog will sit when told in at least 3 different contexts or locations, then the food treat will be offered only occasionally. This is called a variable reinforcement schedule.

Once the sit is easily obtained with a hand signal, you will add the verbal cue. The syntax is as follows: Say "Sit" in a pleasant tone of voice. Pause. Present the old cue (hand signal) as a "helper." Pause. Assess the behaviour–Did the dog sit? If he did, mark it with "Yes" and deliver the food treat. As soon as you can predict the dog will approach you and offer the sit, as you see the dog beginning to sit: Say "Sit" and mark the behaviour with "Yes" and deliver the food treat. Use both of these techniques and soon you will have the sit on a verbal cue.

Timing is crucial! You must mark the behaviour as soon as the dog's bottom hits the ground. Use your reward mark—it is your good friend in communicating what you like to your student. Follow the mark with the food treat. Remember that training treats are tiny—half the size of your little fingernail. And the treats must be something your dog likes and will work for.

Dogs learn by being successful. Please follow these steps carefully. By doing so, you will not teach bad habits and you will also progress very quickly, making the activity fun for you and the dog and avoiding frustration at the same time.

Use the sit every chance you get—before you throw a toy, before you feed Spot dinner, before you pet Spot or play with him, etc. Dogs learn the relevance of obedience when they practice it in daily life. Once you can elicit the sit you can begin the sit/stay. The sit itself does not have to be on a verbal cue yet.

First: Teach the Sit

Sitting for Food/Adding the Verbal Cue: Play first and get the dog excited. When the dog is excited and bouncing around, hold the ball out of reach and say "Sit." As soon as the dog sits, throw the ball. Play a minute, then do another sit. Repeat 3 to 5 times. Then consider the lesson finished.

Next: Begin the Stay Work

Solving stay problems requires predictability of success for the dog. The first stays are in distraction-free locations. When first teaching the stay, do not get into a struggle over the sit. Consider them two different exercises to be strung together later. Just get the sit, by lure or lifting very slightly on the collar, and work on a quick sit some other time. Now, with the dog in sit, keep a steady but slow and controlled stream of food flowing so that this puzzle is initially very easy for your dog to solve. As you progress over the next few days, stretch out the amount of time that you deny the reward. The dog is clear on this exercise when he demonstrates patience no matter how much you move the food or how long you make him wait for it. Work up to two minutes.

what you do	possible reinforcement schedule (just as an example)	date no. of times successful/times attempted
Count:1	Mark It and Feed It ("Yes"—deliver treat) Tip: I allow the dog to eat his treat; usually when he is done he will look up at me. At that point I remind him : "Stay." This begins my next trial.	
2	Mark It and Feed It	
3	Mark It and Feed It	
4	Mark It and Feed It	
5	RM ("Yes" only)	
7	Mark It and Feed It	
4	Mark It and Feed It	
10	RM	
3	Mark It and Feed It	
8	RM	
15	Mark It and Feed It	
7	RM	
3	Mark It and Feed It	
12	Mark It and Feed It	
15	Mark It and Feed It	
7	RM	
18	Mark It and Feed It	
3	RM	
15	Mark It and Feed It	
7	Mark It and Feed It	
20	Mark It and Feed It	
5	RM	
20	Mark It and Feed It	

Work up in this manner to 60 seconds.

Positive Reinforcement

Each step is intended to be performed two or three times. If you can successfully do three steps in a row, move to the next step. If, after six tries you still can't do the next step, back up a step and repeat that one six more times. Then quit. Begin one step back from where you left off to begin the next session.

Distance Work

Now it's time for the dog to learn that stay means that the handler will be right back.

The dog can only learn calmness if he feels that the stay causes the handler to return. Make sure you give the command, "Stay" before you even begin to move away from the dog. Pay close attention to his body language. Any nervousness, licking, or submissiveness means he is not stable about staying in the sit position. You are looking for and reinforcing commitment here. Catch any "breaks" with a no reward mark, then take the dog back to the location and place him back into a sit using steady but gentle upward pressure on the collar. You don't need to jerk, just make him a tiny bit uncomfortable and wait him out. Spot will get tired of being uncomfortable and comply. Don't chatter and talk at the dog. This just muddies the water, confusing him.

As you move, remind Spot to "Stay" as long as he is still getting it right. This helps the dog to know he is on the right track and that he is still getting it right. A command repeated in this context is called a reminder antecedent. If the dog looks like he's going to get up, throw the NRM at him. An NRM is done in a neutral tone. If you cannot do that, then do not use it at all! The sooner you catch the break, the more quickly the dog will figure it out. It is best if you can catch the intention behaviour of getting up and hit it with an NRM. If the dog begins to get up, give an NRM and when the dog lies back, say "Sit," mark it, and feed it. If the dog begins to get up and remembers on his own to stay, mark it and feed it. These are very important concepts for the dog. When you pass behind the dog, it is a big

Once your dog can perform the sit command, start to work on the stay, gradually lengthening the time and distance that he remains in position.

what you do	possible reinforcement schedule (just as an example)	date no. of times successful/times attempted
Now dance: One step left and return	MI & FI (Mark It and Feed It)	
One step right and return	RM (Reward Mark)	
One step back and return	MI & FI	
Two steps left	RM	
Two steps right	MI & FI	
Two steps back	RM—Stop and play a game	
Three steps right	MI & FI	
Three steps left	MI & FI	
Three steps back	RM	
Count 10 in front of the dog	RM—Game	
Two steps right, count 10	MI & FI	
Two steps left, count 10	RM	
Two steps back, count 10	RM	
Five steps right	MI & FI	
Five steps back	RM	
Five steps left	MI & FI	
One step back, about face	MI & FI	
Two steps back, about face	MI & FI	
Three steps back, about face	RM	
Count 20	MI & FI	
Ten steps right	RM—Game	
Ten steps left	RM—Game	
Ten steps back, about face	RM	
Count 10	RM	
Ten steps right, count 20	MI & FI	
Ten steps back, count 20, about face	RM	
Count 30	MI & FI	
Ten steps right, count 30	MI & FI	
Ten steps left, count 30	MI & FI	
Ten steps back, count 40	RM—Game	
Count 15	RM	
Fifteen steps back, count 15	RM	
Ten steps right, count 30	MI & FI	
Count 60	MI & FI	
Walk around the dog in a small circle	MI & FI at the first quarter of the circle	
Walk around the dog in two small circles	Reminder Antecedent (Stay) twice, RM three times, Cookie 2 times	
Make the circle bigger, disappearing out of sight for just one second	MI & FI	
Step out of sight, appear after count of 2, remind dog "Stay", and disappear again for count of 3	RM MI & FI	

step for him. When he can allow you to do this without getting up or turning around, he is truly beginning to learn the exercise calmly. Watching him really learn your commands is exciting and gratifying, especially when you can see focused and calm attention to the handler.

Challenges

When the dog can do everything in the chart calmly, it's time to make the behaviour harder. Each time you expose the dog to a new distraction, it is important to be near the dog, just as in the first lesson. This gives the dog some familiar ground to build confidence. Do not make the dog sit/stay for long periods of time. That is too much. If you need to be somewhere for a time longer than three or four minutes, use a down. At this point, the dog understands the basic sit and stay well enough. Now you are ready to begin with distraction work.

The next step is to have a leash on the dog and let the lead drop to the ground as you give the stay command. Bend over and pick up the lead, commanding the dog to "Stay," with every change of body height. Praise the dog softly so he doesn't break. If Spot does any breaking of the stay, back up and repeat a phase where you know the dog feels confident enough to stay put. When you have done 10 reps, with at least 8 of them being in the "good" category, begin to place the dog neutrally by taking him by the collar and physically guiding him into the sit. Avoid jerking him, but don't be friendly either. Be neutral and calm.

Now gently pet the dog as he remains in a sit/stay. Then have a friend pet him. You may have to gently distract your dog at first, being very close by so you can provide a slow constant feed to help the dog succeed.

Take the dog to at least five different locations. Start at the beginning at first (go back to kindergarten). You will find that as you do more and more different locations, you can quickly escalate the steps until you are getting good stays in new locations almost at once. List your five locations.

1.

2.

3.

4.

5.

Practice your sit/stay in a variety of locations and with distractions.

What steps did you begin with each time? How quickly were you able to get "advanced" stay work in each location? For your new locations, please be sure to keep your dog safe. Have a 30-foot line on him so that accidents due to traffic or getting lost are not issues. Remember to be **twice** as reinforcing in your new locations! Be fair. Give your dog the benefit of the doubt if you haven't done your repetitions. However, once the dog has been in the each context for 5 or 10 trials, insist upon compliance. Neutrally—not angrily. We are dog trainers, not raving lunatics. And be ready to apply loads of R+ to correct responses.

I would call the above protocol about the minimum training you would require to have what would be considered a nice, solid sit/stay that the dog understands and has generalized at least a little. If you haven't done your homework, don't expect to see the behaviour miraculously appear when you need it. If you do, please give me the phone number of your genie—I could use it! Most of all, have fun!

the perfect down/stay

Goal

The dog will down on command.

He will stay until released.

Concepts for the Dog to Understand

Length of time to stay.

Distance.

Resisting distraction.

Crash Course on Learning Theory as it Applies to the Down

You will initially use a primary reinforcer (food) to elicit the behaviour in the form of a "lure." You will also use the food to associate a specific word with meaning, like "That's it!" This word is your reward mark. The words "Yes" or "Good" work well as a reward mark. A reward mark becomes very meaningful to your dog as it gives him information. Concise communication is the name of the game.

You will use a no reward mark, such as "Too bad" or "Try again" to signal to the dog that you don't want the behaviour he is currently offering. Do *not* deliver the food treat. Do not use the word "No," because it is probably already overused in communication between you and your pet.

Initially, the food treat is offered *every time* the down is accomplished. At the point that you can bet me 10 bags of dog food that the dog will down when told in at least 3 different contexts or locations, then the food treat will be offered only occasionally. This is called an intermittent reinforcement schedule.

Once the down is easily obtained with a hand signal, you will add the verbal cue. The syntax is as follows: Say "Down" in a pleasant tone of voice. Pause. Present the old cue (hand signal) as a "helper." Pause. Assess the behaviour: did the dog down? If he did, mark it with "Yes," and deliver the food treat. Or as soon as you can predict your dog will approach you and offer the down, as you see your dog beginning to down say, "Down" and mark the behaviour with "Yes" and deliver the food treat.

Your dog should learn that the stay command means that the handler will be right back. He will only be comfortable staying if he is confident that you will return.

Planning is the most important part of your training sessions.

Use both of these techniques and soon you will have the down on a verbal cue.

Timing is crucial! You must mark the behaviour as soon as your dog's elbows (and bottom) hit the ground. Use your reward mark—it is your good friend in communicating what you like to your student. Follow the mark with the food treat.

Remember that training treats are tiny—half the size of your little fingernail. Also, the treats must be something your dog likes and will work for.

Dogs learn by being successful. Please follow these steps carefully. By doing so you will not teach bad habits and you will also progress very quickly, making the activity fun for you and your dog and avoiding frustration at the same time. Use your down every chance you get—before you throw a toy, before you feed Spot dinner, before you pet Spot or play with him, etc. Dogs learn the relevance of obedience when they practice it in daily life.

Once you can elicit the down you can begin the down/stay. The down itself does not have to be on a verbal cue yet.

First: Teach the Down
Downing for Food/Adding the Verbal Cue

Follow the steps outlined above. When you can elicit the behaviour easily, add the verbal cue-pause-helper prompt sequence.

Play first and get your dog excited. When your dog is playing and jumping around, say "Down." As soon as your dog executes the down, mark the behaviour with a reward mark and then throw the ball, toy, or give a treat. Play a minute, then do another down. Repeat three to five times. Then consider the lesson finished.

Next: Begin the Stay Work

Solving stay problems requires the predictability of success for your dog. The first stays are in distraction-free locations. Now, place your dog into a down. Keep a steady but slow and controlled stream of food flowing so that this puzzle is initially very easy for your dog to solve. As you progress over the next few days, stretch out the amount of time that you deny the reward. Your dog is clear on this exercise when he demonstrates patience no matter how much you move the food or how long you make him wait for it. Work up to two minutes.

Each step is intended to be performed two or three times. If you can successfully do three steps in a row, move to the next step. If after six tries you still can't do the next step, back up a step and repeat that one six more times. Then quit. Begin one step back from where you left off to begin the next session.

Distance Work

Now it's time for your dog to learn that "Stay" means that the handler will be right back. Your dog can only learn calmness if he feels that the stay causes the return of the handler.

Make sure you give the stay command before you even begin to move away from your dog. Pay close attention to his body language. Any nervousness, licking, submissiveness, or lots of tail wagging means he is not stable about staying in the down position. Catch any breaks with a no reward mark, then take your dog back to the location and place him back into a down position using the collar. Neutrally and gently pull straight down on the collar or lure your dog back into position, using a food treat.

what you do	possible reinforcement schedule (just as an example)	date no. of times successful/times attempted
Count to: 1	Mark It and Feed It	
2	Mark It and Feed It	
3	Mark It and Feed It	
4	Mark It and Feed It	
5	RM	
7	Mark It and Feed It	
4	Mark It and Feed It	
10	RM	
3	Mark It and Feed It	
8	RM	
15	Mark It and Feed It	
7	RM	
3	Mark It and Feed It	
12	Mark It and Feed It	
15	Mark It and Feed It	
7	RM	
18	Mark It and Feed It	
3	RM	
15	Mark It and Feed It	
7	Mark It and Feed It	
20	Mark It and Feed It	
5	RM	
20	Mark It and Feed It	

what you do	possible reinforcement schedule (just as an example)	date no. of times attempted no. of times completed
Now dance: One step left and return	MI & FI (Mark It and Feed It)	
One step right and return	RM (Reward Mark)	
One step back and return	MI & FI	
Two steps left	RM	
Two steps right	MI & FI	
Two steps back	RM—Stop and play a game	
Three steps right	MI & FI	
Three steps left	MI & FI	
Three steps back	RM	
Count 10 in front of the dog	RM—Game	
Two steps right, count 10	MI & FI	
Two steps left, count 10	RM	
Two steps back, count 10	RM	
Five steps right	MI & FI	
Five steps back	RM	
Five steps left	MI & FI	
One step back, about face	MI & FI	
Two steps back, about face	MI & FI	
Three steps back, about face	RM	
Count 20	MI & FI	
Ten steps right	RM—Game	
Ten steps left	RM—Game	
Ten steps back, about face	RM	
Count 10	RM	
Ten steps right, count 20	MI & FI	
Ten steps back, count 20, about face	RM	
Count 30	MI & FI	
Ten steps right, count 30	MI & FI	
Ten steps left, count 30	MI & FI	
Ten steps back, count 40	RM-Game	
Count 15	RM	
Fifteen steps back, count 15	RM	
Ten steps right, count 30	MI & FI	
Count 60	MI & FI	
Walk around the dog in a small circle	MI & FI at the first quarter of the circle	
Walk around the dog in two small circles	Reminder Antecedent (Stay) twice, RM three times, Cookie 2 times	
Make the circle bigger, disappearing out of sight for just one second	MI & FI	
Step out of sight, appear after count of 2, remind dog "Stay", and disappear again for count of 3	RM MI & FI	

Don't jerk. Be patient. Don't chatter and talk at your dog. This just muddies the water, confusing him.

As you move, remind Spot to "Stay" as long as he is still getting it right. This helps Spot to know he is on the right track and that he is still getting it right. A command repeated in this context is called a reminder antecedent. If Spot looks like he's going to get up, throw the NRM at him. The sooner you catch the break, the more quickly your dog will figure it out. It is best if you can catch the intention behaviour of getting up and hit it with an NRM. If your dog begins to get up, and you give an NRM and your dog lies back down, mark and feed it. If your dog begins to get up and remembers on his own to stay, mark it and feed it. These are very important concepts for your dog. When you walk behind your dog, it is a big step for him. When he can allow you to do this without getting up or turning around, he is truly beginning to learn the exercise calmly. Watching him really learn your commands is exciting and gratifying.

Challenges

When your dog can do all of the above calmly, it's time to make the behaviour harder. Each time you expose your dog to a new distraction it is important to be near your dog, just as in the first lesson. This gives Spot some familiar ground to build confidence. At this point, your dog understands the basic down and stay well enough. Now you are ready to begin with distraction work.

The next step is to have a leash on your dog and let the lead drop to the ground as you give the stay command. Bend over and pick up the lead, commanding a stay with every change of body height. Praise softly so your dog doesn't break.

If Spot does any breaking of the stay, back up and repeat a phase where you know the dog feels confident enough to stay put. When you have done 10 reps, with at least 8 of them being in the "good" category, begin to place the dog neutrally by taking him by the collar and physically guiding him into the down position. Avoid jerking him. Be neutral.

Now gently pet your dog as he remains in a down/stay. Then have a friend pet him. You may have to gently distract him at first, being close enough to provide a slow and constant feed to help Spot succeed. If Spot persists in getting up even with the constant feed, step on the leash.

Take the dog to at least five different locations. Start at the beginning at first. You will find that as you do more and more different locations, you can quickly escalate the steps until you are getting good stays in new locations almost at once. List your five locations.

1.

2.

3.

4.

5.

Don't stop here. I have taught my dogs to lie down in the living room and remain there while Steve, Abbey, and I prepare dinner, set the table, and eat. I can get up to 45 minutes on one command for this context. At my house the R+ is allowing them to come beg at the table after they have been given the release command. However, you can use any other sort of R+ that you like. Also, initially plan on getting up and placing Spot where you want him to remain each time he breaks and also getting up to give him a food treat for remaining in place. So the first, say, five sessions plan on eating cold dinner and being interrupted a lot. If you have many family members, you can assign one night per person or something like that.

basic doggie
cookie recipe

From the Kitchen and Kennel of Sherrie Start.
Thanks Sherrie, you culinary genius!

Ingredients

2 cups oatmeal

3-4 cups whole wheat flour

$1\,^1/_2$ cups of other flour (rice, rye, or corn meal)

$^1/_2$ cup oil

2 eggs

Water to firm—roll-out type consistency

Special ingredients

pumpkin with allspice, cinnamon, or nutmeg

apple sauce

carob

peanut butter

maple syrup (also a topping)

barbecue sauce (also a topping)

grated cheese

salmon

bouillon

nuts

Directions

Soak oatmeal in 2 cups water for 5 minutes.

Add oil and eggs.

Mix well.

Stir in 1 cup "other flour" and 3 cups whole wheat flour.

Add ingredients from **special ingredients** list.

Mix well.

Alternate mixing in water and flour until dough is slightly dry and will hold together.

Dump onto well-floured surface.

Knead, adding flour as needed until dough is no longer sticky.

Roll out to about 1/2" thickness and cut into desired shapes.

Bake at 325 degrees F for 1 hour.

Turn oven off and leave several hours or overnight.

If cookies are not "bone hard," turn oven back on to bake and let warm to 325 degrees.

Turn off and let cool again.

appendix
suggested reading

Video Materials

The Power of Positive Series, Patty Ruzzo, Leslie Nelson, and Ted Turner

Positively Fetching, Adele Yunck and Judy Byron

Patient Like the Chipmunks, Bob Bailey and Marion Breland-Bailey

Clicker Magic, Karen Pryor

Books

Finding a Balance, Suzanne Clothier

Self Control, Suzanne Clothier

Body Posture and Emotions, Suzanne Clothier

Seven C's, Suzanne Clothier

The Thirdway, Chris Bach

These items are all available through Direct Book Service:

509-663-9115

Box 2778 701B Poplar

Wenatchee, WA 98801

glossary

antecedent

Going before or preceeding. Any occurrence or event prior to another.

associative learning

To associate means to connect or join together, to combine, to connect in the mind. Associative learning means that your dog relies primarily on the events immediately surrounding their behaviour or events occurring concurrently (during) the behaviour to make decisions about whether that was a good behaviour to repeat or a behaviour that will be decreased in the future.

aversive

Any event, context, or circumstance that one wishes to avoid. An aversive event is a stimulus that would suppress a behaviour that it follows or a stimulus that would increase a behaviour, where that behaviour would terminate the aversive.

backtraining

A specific method of linking separate behaviours into one behaviour sequence. In backtraining, the last behaviour in the sequence would be taught first, then the next to last, and so on. This way the animal is moving from unknown into known behaviours. See also chain, chaining, behaviour sequences.

behaviour

Any observable or measurable response or act. Any overt (externally observable) activity.

behaviour modification protocol

A protocol is a preliminary draft or record of a transaction. A behaviour modification protocol refers to the specific, methodical steps one would follow to change a specific behaviour or set of behaviours.

behaviour sequences

Any time you link several behaviours together to make a related or continuous series of behaviours, you are creating a behaviour sequence. The individual behaviours would follow one after the other to form a complete exercise. For example, the formal obedience recall consists of several separate behaviours linked together to form a logical sequence. See also backtraining, chaining, chain.

blocking

When a new command and an old command are given simultaneously, the known command is more salient, or noticed by your dog. See also overshadowing.

bridge

A synonym for reward mark. See also secondary reinforcer, reward mark, bridge.

chain

A sequence of behaviours that occurs in a fixed pattern. Over time, each behaviour in the sequence or series becomes a cue or stimulus to perform the next behaviour in the sequence. In the same manner, each behaviour, excepting the first one, becomes a conditioned reinforcer for the behaviour preceding it. See also chain, behaviour sequence, backtraining.

chaining

Developing a sequence of responses in reverse order. In this way, one can develop a complex series of behaviours by teaching the last one first.

classical conditioning

A type of learning where respondent behaviours are brought under the control of otherwise neutral or previously meaningless stimuli. Also known as respondent conditioning. In short, new stimuli can elicit respondent behaviour.

clicker

A small plastic device with a metal tab that makes a "click-click" sound when activated. Because this is a unique sound in the environment, it makes an excellent and salient R+ for our dogs, cats, horses, goats, and other animals.

competing reinforcers

The rivalry that occurs when all you have is praise and your dog sees a squirrel. The dog goes for the activity or situation that looks like the most fun.

conditioned reinforcer

An event or stimulus that becomes reinforcing through learning. This event/stimulus is not reinforcing until it is paired with other events that are already known reinforcers. The best way to obtain a conditioned reinforcer is to pair your stimulus (such as a word or a clicker) with food, which is a primary reinforcer. See also secondary reinforcer, reward mark, bridge.

conditioned response

A response that is elicited by a specific cue or context. This resembles an unconditioned response, but is not identical to it. The difference being that the conditioned response involves learned behaviours rather than fixed action patterns (instinctive behaviours). For a conditioned response to occur, a conditioned stimulus is paired with an unconditioned stimulus. After a period of time, the behaviour is apparent in the presence of the conditioned stimulus even when the unconditioned stimulus is not present.

conflict resolution

Conflict resolution has to do with coming to terms with a specific disagreement, so that all parties involved can amicably behave in a fashion that works for all of those involved. When dealing with animals, the onus is upon us, the humans, to resolve conflict in a peaceful and nonconfrontational manner.

consequent events

An event that logically or naturally follows an action. A result or an effect.

contingency relationships

The relationship between a behaviour (response) and the antecedent (events that precede the behaviour) or the consequences (events that follow the behaviour).

contingent events

Events that can be linked directly to the specified behaviour. For instance, contingent delivery of a reinforcer would indicate that the R+ is given only in the presence of a specific behaviour.

discrimination

Responding differently in the presence of different antecedent events or cues. It's part of how dogs "find Waldo," so that they can establish the pattern.

fading

Removing, methodically and gradually, additional prompts, modeling (physical guidance), and extra cues from the antecedents required to elicit the behaviour. See also prompts.

fear

Fear is a very primal emotion. Fear can be so intense as to prevent learning at all. Fear is specifically: A feeling of alarm or disquiet caused by the expectation of danger, pain, or disaster; to feel anxious or apprehensive about a situation or context. Please note the "expectation." What may not look fear-inducing to you certainly may look fear-inducing to your dog, or another human for that matter.

first events

First events are significant because of the effect first events have on memory. First events are often remembered with great clarity. Make certain that your dog is getting the "first impression" that you want him to have.

generalization

In dog training, generalization has to do specifically with transferring a behaviour intact from one context into another.

inter-command discrimination

The ability to tell the difference between cues and therefore respond correctly in the presence of different cues. In other words, the dog has made the connection—he knows which cue belongs to which behaviour.

latency

Technically, latency is "latent period," which means the interval between a stimulus and a response. In behavioural literature this is often referred to as merely "latency" and is defined as: the time lapse between the presentation of a stimulus and the occurrence of the behaviour. For example, if you give your dog a cue, the latency is the time it takes the dog to respond to the stimulus (cue). Once the dog has responded, it is a cue for you to respond with a consequence—how quickly you respond is also defined as latency. The only rule with latency is to make it as small as you possibly can.

learned behaviours
An acquired wisdom, knowledge, or skill. If fixed action patterns (instinctive behaviour) are the resident software and reflexes are the hard-wired (type behaviours), learned behaviours are the peripheral software that greatly increases the usefulness of your computer. Learned behaviours are attained through life experience, valuable information, indeed!

manufactured behaviour
In the dictionary it means "to make or process a raw material into a finished product." Here it means that behaviour not naturally offered up by the student must be obtained somehow so it can be reinforced, so it will occur again. You, the trainer, elicit behaviour from the student by using lures, prompts, physical guiding, and other methods of shaping. In short, the trainer manufactures a response so that he has the opportunity to apply R+.

memory markers
Memory is the mental capability to retain and recall past experiences. A memory marker is an event or stimulus that would aid in the retention of an experience so that it is more easily recalled.

negative punishment
The removal of an item that the trainee wishes to have, the result of that action being a decrease in the frequency of that particular response.

negative reinforcement
The removal of an aversive event, resulting in an increase in the frequency of that particular response. The desirable response should serve as a switch to "turn off" the aversive event.

NRM
No reward mark.

operant behaviour
Offered behaviour that is directly controlled by the consequences contingent on that behaviour.

operant conditioning
A specific type of learning in which behaviours are altered or changed primarily by manipulating the consequences that follow them.

opportunity training
If you see your dog offering unsolicited, but wonderful, desirable behaviour, give him social approval, an RM, a cookie, and/or other R+. That way, you'll get to see that great behaviour again. It also sets the scene for modifying some behaviours. It's easier to communicate to your dog that this behaviour won't do if he has a clue about what might be an acceptable alternative.

overshadowing
When two cues are presented to the dog simultaneously, one will be noticed more than the other. See also blocking.

P+, P-
Shorthand for positive punishment, negative punishment, respectively.

positive punishment

A decrease in the frequency of a behaviour that is followed by an aversive event.

positive reinforcement

An increase in the frequency of a behaviour that is followed by an event or stimulus that the trainee wants to have or receive (postive reinforcer).

primary reinforcers

Required for survival. Food, water, air. Sex is listed in some literature, other behaviourists feel that sex should not be included as a primary reinforcer.

prompts

Antecedent events that aid in initiating a response. An additional cue that helps elicit a specific response. Gestures, lures, and additional cues all serve as prompts. See also fading.

protocol

In the dictionary it means any preliminary draft or record of a transaction. To a behaviourist, a protocol is the map of a behaviour modification program. The protocol sets the program down on paper, in a step-by-step fashion, usually relying upon successive approximation as a core technique. The protocol is used by the behaviourist as the big picture and the details. It is also used by the client as a guideline.

punishment

Application of an aversive event or removal of an R+ event with the result being that there is a decrease in the frequency of the target behaviour. Punishment causes avoidance behaviour and can encourage aggression in specific circumstances.

R+, R-

Shorthand for positive reinforcement, negative reinforcement, respectively.

reinforcement

Adding an event that the trainee (dog) wants to have happen again or removal of an aversive event, the results being that there is an increase in the frequency of the target behaviour.

reinforcement history

Each behaviour will have a history of R+ and other kinds of feedback. Also, each individual will have a history of experiences that he has had with others. The sum of those experiences could be called the reinforcement history.

reinforcement schedules

The rules or guidelines one uses to determine how many and which responses will receive how many and which reinforcers. Basically, there are four kinds: fixed ratio, fixed interval, variable ratio, and variable interval. Ratio refers to how much of the R+ is given. Interval refers to how often the R+ is given. An intermittent schedule refers to a type of variable schedule in which only some occurences of a behaviour are R+, usually the "best efforts."

When developing a behaviour, a fixed schedule (1 behaviour = 1 R+) is the rule. To maintain behaviour that the animal already knows, a variable schedule (variable ratio, variable interval, and intermittent schedule with reinforcement variety) is the schedule you use.

respondent

Behaviour that is controlled or elicited by antecedent stimuli. Reflexes are respondents because their performance automatically and predictably occurs in the presence of specific cues or contexts. The correlation between these unconditioned respondents and the antecedent events that control them is an unlearned response. See also classical conditioning.

response

A reply or answer. For animal trainers, it is a reaction of the animal to a specific stimulus.

reward mark

A reward mark tells your dog that you liked a behaviour and wish to see it again. An RM is a precise way to communicate to your dog what you like about the behaviour he is offering you. See also secondary reinforcer, conditioned reinforcer, bridge.

RM

Reward mark.

salient

The event or stimulus that is most noticed or most conspicuous.

satiation

Too much of a good thing. If you provide an excessive amount of a reinforcer you may find that the reinforcer has temporarily lost its effectiveness.

secondary reinforcer

See also conditioned reinforcer, reward mark, bridge.

setting events

Those antecedent events that refer to context, conditions, or other situations that will have an affect on the antecedent-behaviour-consequence relationship. Setting events are often present in the environment, so prepare for them! Setting events can have a big influence on the behaviour you see, therefore the consequence provided.

shaping

Developing a behaviour toward an end goal, specifically using successive approximation as a technique to get there. Successive approximation is the process of breaking the terminal response or end goal behaviour down into many tiny steps or "approximations." You learn to count, then add, subtract, multiply, and divide before you learn calculus and statistical mathematics.

spoil

Term means to prevent direct access or prevent access to the dog reinforcing himself. If the dog takes off after a squirrel and gets to chase it, he has reinforced his disobedience to the come command. What you do when you catch him will probably alter the behaviour little, depending upon just how reinforcing the dog finds squirrel chasing. In this case, you must "spoil" the squirrel chasing.

stress

A mental, emotional, and physical reaction to distress. Stress can prevent learning. Stress is also always present in the environment to some degree and must be dealt with. Teach your dog to be resilient under stress. Please read *On Talking Terms with Dogs*, by Turid Rugaas.

successive approximation

See shaping.

target behaviour

The behaviour you are currently focusing on, modifying, changing, or shaping.

terminal response

The end goal. The finished picture. The behaviour or behaviour sequence that you want to get when you have applied all of this great training advice, specifically shaping. A terminal response is the end or final result of shaping behaviour.

thin schedule

How much behaviour you can get for the least amount of reinforcement.

timing

The lapse of time between the animal offering a behaviour or response and the trainers reaction to that response: The quicker the better!

training treats

Treats must be tiny! Use lots of treats up front to modify behaviour, less as you place the behaviour on a variable schedule.

unconditioned response

A response that is evoked by a stimulus before being taught or learned. We don't have to "learn" that food and water are good for us, we know they are. If the doctor hits your knee in the right area with that nasty little hammer, your leg reacts in a reflexive manner. Unconditioned responses used to be called unconditioned reflex.

undertraining

What the majority of our dogs suffer from! Undertraining is not enough training in enough different circumstances: too few repetitions, not enough trials, inadequate number of locations, etc. Basically, you haven't done the vast quantity of rote repetitions required for the behaviour to become a habit, a learned behaviour.

appendix references

Seminars

Jean Donaldson

Judy Howard

Karen Pryor

Patty Ruzzo

Ted Turner

Leslie Nelson

Chris Bach

Books

American Heritage Dictionary.

Behan, Kevin, *Natural Dog Training*. NY: William and Morrow Co., Inc., 1992.

Booth, Sheila, with Dildei, Gottfried, *Schutzhund Obedience—Training in Drive*. Ridgefield, CT: Podium Publications, 1992.

Chance, Paul, *Learning and Behavior*. Pacific Grove, CA: Brooks/Cole, 1994.

Donaldson, Jean, *The Culture Clash*. Berkeley, CA: James & Kenneth, 1996.

Fisher, John, *Reinforcement Training for Dogs*, 1992.

Fogle, Dr. Bruce, *Know Your Dog, An Owner's Guide to Dog Behavior*. New York, NY: Dorling Kindersley, 1992.

Kazdin, Alan, *Behavior Modification in Applied Settings,* 1994.

Martin, Garry and Pear, Joseph, *Behavior Modification, What It Is and How to Do It*. NJ: Prentice Hall, 1996.

Mitchell, Lana, *Click! For Success*. Hillsboro, OR: Lana Mitchell, 1997.

Pryor, Karen, *Don't Shoot the Dog—The New Art of Teaching and Training*. NY: Bantam, 1985.

Reid, Pamela J., Ph.D., *Excelerated Learning*. Oakland, CA: James & Kenneth, 1996.

Rogerson, John, *The Instructor's Manual*. Wenatchee, WA: Direct Book Service, 1992.

Rugaas, Turid, *On Talking Terms with Dogs: Calming Signals*. Kula, HI: Legacy by Mail, Inc., 1997.

Sidman, Murray, *Coercion and Its Fallout*. Boston, MA: Authors Cooperative, Inc., 1989.

Volhard, Joachim and Fisher, Gail Tamases, *Training Your Dog—Step by Step*. New York: Howell Book House, 1983.

Weston, David, *Dog Training—The Gentle Modern Method*. NY: Howell Book House, 1990.

index

photo credits